FIX YOUR BODY, FIX YOUR SWING

FIX YOUR BODY,

FIX

The Revolutionary Biomechanics

YOUR

Workout Program Used by Tour Pros

SWING

JOEY DIOVISALVI
AND
STEVE STEINBERG

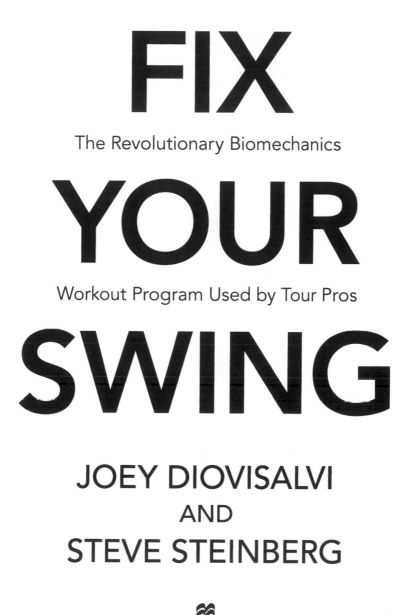

St. Martin's Press

NEW YORK

www.stmartins.com

Book design by Level C

Library of Congress Cataloging-in-Publication Data

Diovisalvi, Joey.
    Fix your body, fix your swing : the revolutionary biomechanics workout program used by tour pros / Joey Diovisalvi and Steve Steinberg.
          p. cm.
    ISBN 978-0-312-60562-9
    1. Swing (Golf) 2. Golf—Physiological aspects. 3. Physical fitness. I. Steinberg, Steve. II. Title.
    GV979.S9D56 2010
    796.352'3—dc22

                                                        2009033516

10   9   8   7   6   5   4   3

Contents

Acknowledgments

Thanks to Steve Cohen, Marc Resnick, and everyone at St. Martin's Press for believing and trusting in what this book is about. To Greg Hopkins and Cleveland Golf for having the vision to see the impact that biomechanics would have on the sport of golf. To my very good friend Vijay Singh for inspiring me to truly learn to understand golf at such a deep level. This book would not exist had it not been for Vijay's dedication to the game. To Jason Dufner, Jason Gore, Ryuji Imada, Pat Perez, Travis Perkins, Tom Pernice Jr., John Rollins, Charlie Wi, and Tim Wilkinson. To Sophie Gustafson, Zach Johnson, Davis Love III, Jim Nantz, and Ian Poulter. To Todd Jones and everyone at the PGA Tour Academy at TPC Sawgrass for allowing me to teach at such an elite level. And to the PGA Tour for being such an instrumental part of my life and career over the last ten years.

—Joey Diovisalvi, June 2009

Thanks to Joey Diovisalvi for opening up his home to me, letting me help him deliver his message, and—most importantly—becoming a good friend. To his players for being so accessible and candid. To the people at St. Martin's Press for being so helpful and easy to work with. And thanks to these folks for contributions large and small: Andre, Cherie, Don, Erin, Justin, Michele, Patrick, and Sabunim.

—Steve Steinberg, June 2009

Foreword

First off, I'm you. I run a business. As the CEO of Cleveland Golf, I'm a busy guy. You may not actually run a company, but you have a job. And you're busy.

I'm also you because I'm a golfer and I'm a dreamer.

When I turned forty-seven, my body started falling apart. That's what it does when you're forty-seven. Dreams die hard, though. I was forty-seven and I wanted to play professional golf . . . somehow . . . somewhere. I knew I couldn't compete with the kids that were playing on the PGA Tour, but fifty was right around the corner—that magical fifty mark—and I decided that I wanted to play on a senior tour.

I knew Joey through Vijay Singh. Vijay was one of Cleveland Golf's most accomplished touring professionals. I had witnessed firsthand what Joey had done with him and saw the phenomenal things that Vijay was doing. I, of course, had no idea what any of the stuff they were doing together was about.

My wife, Dr. Linda Hopkins, however, did. She's a triathlete. She runs those absolutely insane Ironman Triathlons (not just those semi-insane sprint triathlons). She and Joey spoke the same language. She understood all about Joey's use of biomechanical assessments and golf-specific exercises. "You need to listen to what Joey is talking about," she said. "You really should pay attention to this." She had connected the dots before I did because she understood the science. I'm not stupid, though, so I can connect the dots quickly enough if you put them directly in front of me. Most businessmen can.

Soon after, I found myself talking with Vijay and Joey at the Ritz-Carlton in Maui. My interest in what they were doing was twofold. I was watching one of Cleveland Golf's top players get better and better and better with no end in sight. I was also—more selfishly—trying to figure out if I could benefit from these same techniques. Later on, Joey and I ended up talking about goals. He asked what my goals were, and—let's face it—I had a lofty and unlikely dream. Slightly embarrassed, I told him that I was hoping to get a tour card somewhere. He knew I had some decent skills, but I was expecting him to say, "Sure you want a tour card. So does everyone else in the world." Instead, he looked at me and told me I could do it . . . and then he told me what it would involve.

We started working together and I saw pretty quickly that I was going in the right direction. I put in a hell of a lot of hard work and learned a lot about how the body needs to be able to move in order to be successful in golf. And I ended up getting my European Seniors Tour card. I got to play in Japan and on the Champions Tour. Because of business commitments, I can't play a full tour schedule. I can, though, live my dream and compete in five, six, or seven events a year. I'm fifty-three years old now, and my body is allowing me to play at a professional level.

I'm in better shape today—more flexible, stronger, more mobile—at fifty-three than I was at thirty. I'm also swinging the golf club the way I did when I was twenty-five. As my wife, Linda, says, the golf ball doesn't know how old I am. I'd like to say it's all equipment-related—heck, I'd be negligent as an equipment manufacturer not to try to plant that idea in your head—but it's probably more biomechanics-related.

To me, the assessments and exercises that Joey prescribes are as big a part of what I do in golf as practicing my chipping and putting. It's interwoven. When I go to the gym to work on the things we've talked about, it's just like hitting golf balls. It's part of the process. It's got into my DNA. And there's no reason you can't take the things in this book and see where they lead you. I can't guarantee you'll end up doing what I did, but there's no reason you can't win your club championship.

This is why I wanted to be a part of this book. Because of who I am, I get asked to write the foreword for golf books all the time. This is the first one I've ever done. I never wanted to be a part of something that wasn't the truth and that I didn't truly believe in.

I'm not a top name on the PGA Tour. You may respect those golfers and want to play like them, but you can't really relate to them. They're on TV. They're larger-than-life. But I'm the average guy. I play golf every Saturday morning with my buds. You've never heard of me.

I'm the common golfer. I'm Greg Hopkins—a guy that had a dream. I'm a businessman. If you're sitting reading this in your office between meetings or during a rushed five-minute lunch break, I'm you. You're me. We're the same person. We're golfers and we're dreamers.

Everyone has his own pot of gold. Everyone has his own endgame that he's after. But you'll never get there unless you have a process—and this is the process. This isn't sleight of hand. This is something that's attainable.

And there's nobody that can tell me that he can't do it, because—well—I've done it.

—GREG HOPKINS
CEO, Cleveland Golf
European Seniors Tour professional
January 2009

Introduction

At last count, approximately 20 billion different golf books were out there. That's right: there are roughly three books about golf for every man, woman, and child on the planet Earth.

As people, do we really need number 20 billion and one?

I think so—and in about four paragraphs, so will you.

Typical golf training is like the medical industry in this country—we tend to treat symptoms rather than causes. You go to the doctor because you're having trouble sleeping and he gives you a prescription. A month later, you find yourself up all night again and he writes you another prescription. Two months later, you're staring at the ceiling at three in the morning and—surprise—you get another prescription. On the golf course, you take the "perfect swing" that you've put together after reading book after book and magazine article after magazine article, and you still find yourself slicing the ball or lacking power. So, what do you do? You adjust your stance and foot position to take the slice into account, you wrench your shoulders back a few extra—and painful—degrees in an attempt to get more speed in your swing, and you go out and drop $400 on the latest and fanciest driver. Are your drives any more accurate or powerful? Probably not. If anything, they're less consistent than they've ever been—and you're out a few hundred bucks to boot.

To really get rid of your insomnia and to really correct your swing, you have to treat the causes of the problems—not the symptoms. I can't help you sleep any better at night, but I can help your golf game. (And, hey, that might end up helping you sleep better at night.)

As one of the top golf biomechanics coaches in the country, I've worked with everyone from weekend warriors to the top-rated player in the world. (I was part of the team that helped Vijay Singh make it to number one in the world in 2004.) I'm on the road forty weeks a year with my players and have spent—literally—tens of thousands of hours watching and analyzing and correcting swings. Whether you play the game once a month or every day, the same truths apply. You have to fix your body before you can fix your swing.

You need to treat the causes of the problem, not the symptoms.

A lot of the time a bad swing doesn't mean that you're doing things wrong—it's just that your body isn't letting you do things right. You may know exactly what you should be doing, but if your body won't cooperate, that perfect swing can never happen. You might as well try to teach a squirrel how to speak French. I don't care how many times you tell it that *pomme de terre* means "potato," it'll never do anything more than stare at you with that curious, head-tilted-to-the-side squirrel look.

It's the same with your body. If it isn't capable of swinging perfectly, it can't swing perfectly.

The good news is that once you understand the limitations that your body currently has, you'll be able to go in and correct them. Once you've corrected them, your body will be able to do all of those things that the books, magazines, and the pro at your club have been telling you to do. Even the most deep-seated of bad habits can be broken once you determine its cause. Eventually, your old swing will feel as odd and strange as wearing someone else's shoes. This book will help you figure out the underlying causes of your problems so you can take your game to the next level.

If you came to see me at the PGA Tour Academy at TPC Sawgrass in Ponte Vedra, Florida, I could analyze and deconstruct your swing using a ton of expensive and high-tech equipment that's installed there. The equipment is great. It can sense and detect things that the human eye just isn't capable of seeing. But when I'm on the road, I don't have access to these toys. What I do have is an understanding of biomechanics. To analyze the movement patterns of my players, I use the same assessments that are in this book. With these simple biomechanical assessments, I'm able to figure out what parts of the body are weak, tight, or unstable. I then put my players on the same exercise regimens you'll find here.

Once the body is fixed, the swing is fixed.

So what is biomechanics anyway? Biomechanics is the study of how forces exerted both internally (by the muscles) and externally (by gravity) affect the skeletal system. You could study biomechanics to learn how birds fly or how horses run, but I'm obsessed with the biomechanics of golf. Think about it: what parts of the body *aren't* involved in the golf swing? The golf swing is an incredibly complex motion that requires almost every part of the body to work together in harmony. If parts of the body aren't up to the challenge, there's no harmony. The swing suffers and you're in the woods looking for your ball.

Don't worry. This isn't a graduate-level textbook and you won't have to know—or plow through—a bunch of heavy science to be able to use what I'm going to give you. I will go over some of the science behind what I do, but it's mainly to help you understand the concepts. You can even skip over the science parts, but it's there if you want it. Hey, you never know—the next business deal you close on the course may be solely due to your knowing the location and function of the infraspinatus or multifidus muscles. Whether you decide to get into the science or not, the book will give you easy-to-use ways to determine the weaknesses in your body that may be resulting in weaknesses in your game.

The simple tests and simple exercises that you'll find in this book will let you get your body into the condition that it needs to be in to play the game the way you want to play it. And I stress the words *your body*. Because no one will perform identically or get the same results from the assessments, the workouts that you'll be doing will be tailored specifically to your body's issues and concerns. Everyone in your weekly foursome could be reading and using this book, but all four might be doing completely different workouts.

Think of it as a "troubleshooting guide" for the golfer's body. And while this is a golf-specific book—you probably won't get "jacked" or develop a ripped six-pack with these exercises—you may notice some benefits off the course. If you've had lower-back or shoulder trouble, for example, the same drills that'll add distance and accuracy to your drive will help you stay pain-free at home or at the office.

You're about to embark on a very different and cutting-edge fitness program. But you're not going to have to go it alone. In addition to my words of wisdom, you'll also be hearing from a lot of the pros that I work with. We're going to take you into the inner sanctum of twenty-first-century golf training and conditioning. You'll get an insider's view of what goes on behind the scenes of the golf world that you may only know about from watching TV. You'll get firsthand comments from some of the game's best players about how these assessments and exercises have helped them and their games. You'll also get to see them going through the actual workouts. The pictures in the book aren't of professional fitness models; they're of players whose very livelihoods depend on getting their bodies in the condition required to play the game at an elite level.

They know that before you can fix your swing, you have to fix your body.

Now it's your turn.

Let's get to work.

Who Is Joey D.?

or . . . Why Are You Reading This Book?

"Joey D.," Vijay Singh said with a giant smile on his face. "You sounded taller over the phone."

The first time I met Vijay Singh, he insulted me. I instantly liked him.

This was back in 2001. He'd heard some good things about me and thought maybe something about this unorthodox golf coach with some unorthodox training methods could help him take his game to the next level. Vijay and I worked together for a few months, and in March 2002 he notched his first tour victory in almost two years by winning the Shell Houston Open by a comfortable six strokes.

He invited me to fly back to Ponte Vedra, Florida, with him on his plane.

"What would it take to get you to work with me exclusively?" he asked me. Before I could even start to consider the offer, he added, "I know I can be the best player in the world."

In 2002, everyone just assumed that Tiger Woods was invincible and would be number one in the world for as long as the sport of golf interested him. Vijay Singh was a PGA Tour Rookie of the Year in 1993, but had managed just a single tour win since 2000. Here he was, though, telling me that he thought he could be number one. Most people would have laughed at his prediction, but I knew how hard a worker he was. In the time I had been with him, he'd just about kill himself whenever we worked out. I respected his work ethic immensely, but I also knew that trying to overtake Tiger would be going up against some stiff odds. I knew something about facing insurmountable odds, though.

I sold my training facility in south Florida and moved north to Ponte Vedra.

In September 2004, Vijay outshot Tiger Woods and Adam Scott by three strokes to win the Deutsche Bank Championship in Norton, Massachusetts. As a result, he leapfrogged over Tiger and into the number one spot in the world. Thanks to hard work and a team of dedicated and knowledgeable professionals, Vijay had made good on his prediction. In April 2005, when he was elected into the World Golf Hall of Fame, Vijay thanked several people in his acceptance speech. I was one of them. I sometimes wonder what it was that made me uproot my life to go work with him, and I always come back to what he said to me on that flight from Texas: "I know I can be the best player in the world."

Something about his confidence and determination reminded me of someone.

NEW JERSEY

As a kid, I would never accept anything but 100 percent of myself. I played football in junior leagues and developmental leagues, and I recognized early on that I was stronger and faster than the other kids. Physically, I was pretty lucky in my genetics. But mentally, I just approached the game differently from my friends. The way I thought about things was completely different from anybody else's. I'd see things that no one else saw. I recognized I was a leader because I had no fear of anything at all. That could have been a good thing or a bad thing, but it made me relentless in just about anything I did.

I never wanted anyone to drive me to football practice, for example. I wanted to ride my bike to practice because, I used to think, if I rode my bike, I would already be ahead of the curve when I got there. And if we didn't win a game, I would come completely unglued. Everybody would leave to do whatever they did after a game, and I would just stay there doing drills and running for hours. I grew up in Manalapan, New Jersey—a typical suburb in Monmouth County. In the late summer, I knew that football season was right around the corner, and I would run up and down the hills. It'd be light out when I started, and eventually the sun would go down and it would be dark and I'd still be running. It'd be nine at night and I'd still be out there. I used to tell myself, "I need to be faster. I need to be in better shape than anybody else when I get to the first day of practice."

When the season started, I was always in the best shape I could possibly be in. Couple this with my natural skills, and I was a monster on the field. They'd put me on the bench after the first half because I was destroying people. Opposing coaches constantly questioned my age, saying I had to have been much older than I said I was.

I'm not sure where this extreme work ethic came from. I come from an average middle-class family. Everybody worked and everyone had this dream and vision to better himself. You were taught from the beginning that hard work was the key to success—on the field, in the classroom, everywhere. My dad was demanding about grades. If I wasn't on the honor roll, I couldn't play any sports. It drove me to understand the importance of education. And since I was so driven about getting in the best shape I could be in, it was natural for me to start learning as much as I could about how the body worked.

From a young age, I started studying what I could do to make myself a better athlete. I knew it was more than just pure strength—more than just how much I could bench-press or how much I could squat. Being an athlete was about knowing how to use that strength in motion. The strongest guy on the field is just the strongest guy on the field unless he knows how to use that strength in the particular sport that he's playing. By then, I had branched out from just playing football. I had started wrestling and began studying martial arts. I was continually amazed at how these lighter-weight-class wrestlers and my martial arts instructors—at maybe 130 pounds—could do these incredible things with their bodies. They generated the same amount of strength and power and explosiveness as much bigger guys. I started to become obsessed with figuring out where this ability came from. How could these small individuals have this power and transfer it through movement and have such amazing results? In my head, I began to think about how these movements and movement patterns could be applied to other sports with similar results. That's when I started to really understand movement strength.

Unfortunately, both my research and my football career were about to be put on hold.

SETBACKS

Two months before my eighteenth birthday, I was diagnosed with testicular cancer. A biopsy later revealed that the cancer had spread and had developed into lymphatic cancer. Despite all the work I had put into my training and into my body, I had a terminal disease. I saw a ton of doctors and surgeons, and at the end of most of these visits, someone in a white coat with a serious expression on his or her face would ask me what I'd like to do with the next—and final—ten months of my life. All of a sudden, at eighteen years old, everything I had ever dreamed about was gone. It was surreal. All of these specialists were telling me that I was going to die, but I still felt great. I felt as if I could run through walls.

I approached my sickness the way I'd approached just about everything else up to that point in my life. Because of who I was, I wasn't simply going to lie down. I couldn't. It just wasn't part of my makeup. Eventually, I found a doctor who was willing to take a chance on surgery. He told me about an invasive and difficult procedure. He said he was willing to try it because he was convinced I was strong enough to handle it. I thought back to the long and painful hours I'd spent in the gym and running those hills. All that time I thought I had been training for football.

Then the real game began. I went into the hospital and they did all of these extensive tests and scheduled me for major surgery. They told me that the procedure would take a certain number of hours, but when they went in, they found a lot more problems than they expected. I was fighting for my life. I made it through the surgery, but no one was sure if they got all of the cancer or if it had spread somewhere else.

Chemotherapy treatments started and the months started to go by. At the time, chemo wasn't outpatient for most people. I had to be in the hospital seven or ten days at a time. Over a year and a half, I went from a ferocious 218-pound teenager that was going to take the football world apart to an emaciated 140-pound kid. On top of the weight loss, the chemo affected all of my senses. I lost all of my senses. I had no sense of taste. I had no sense of feeling. I had no strength. I was sick constantly. It was a nightmare. But I survived.

Call it destiny, the work of God, whatever. I don't want to get caught up in all of that. My personal belief is that it wasn't really my time to go. With a clean bill of health, I now had to rebuild what was left of my body. I spent the next eighteen months strengthening and reteaching my muscles how to do the things that they used to do so effortlessly and naturally. My body bounced back. (If you're a collector of old muscle magazines, which would immediately make me very suspect of you, check out the August 1991 issue of *Robert Kennedy's Muscle Mag International*. It has a feature on me and my illness, recovery, and subsequent success as a trainer.) At age twenty-two, I had fought back and conquered a terminal illness. My dream of playing college or pro football, though, was gone.

SOUTH FLORIDA

In the mideighties, I moved down to West Palm Beach. I figured that if I had built—and then rebuilt—my body using principles I'd developed, it was time to see how these theories worked on other people. I'd helped out people in the gym all of my life, but Florida would give me access to a different breed of client—the pro athlete. A lot of NBA and NFL guys spend their off-seasons down there, and with around half of the Major League Baseball teams doing their spring training in the surrounding areas, it just seemed like the place to be. The challenge was getting the first few athletes to understand and believe in what I was doing. Once they saw how these methodologies really worked, word spread quickly. I started developing a reputation in the West Palm Beach area as a strength and conditioning coach that got results.

One of the first pro athletes I worked with was Shelton Jones—a former standout basketball player at St. John's University. He was drafted in the second round of the 1988 NBA draft by the San Antonio Spurs and ended up playing the majority of his rookie season with the Philadelphia 76ers. It was a thrill to finally branch out into different sports—to be able to take these things about movement and strength that I'd learned as a kid by wrestling and studying martial arts and use them with this big six-foot-eight-inch basketball player to teach him how to become quicker and more agile on the court.

My work with Shelton led to work with other NBA players, such as Roy Hinson, whose career spanned almost a decade. Then came baseball players such as Tracy Jones, a former first-round pick who had a killer rookie season with the Cincinnati Reds, and Jeff Innis, a pitcher who spent his entire career with the New York Mets. Of course, Florida is also a hotbed for high school and college football. There was no shortage of work getting high school kids ready for the collegiate game and college kids ready for the NFL combines, where they would have one last chance to impress the pro scouts with their talents. It was an incredibly rewarding and fascinating ten years.

BORN TO RUN . . . AND STRETCH . . . AND STRENGTHEN

In the late nineties, my reputation started to expand beyond just the sports world. In 1999, I got a call from Clarence Clemons—the sax player from Bruce Springsteen's E Street Band. He had just had his hip replaced and was looking for someone to work with him on rehab and strengthening during the band's upcoming world tour. So I left my facility to go out on the road helping Clarence. Through him, I met—and start working with—Nils Lofgren. That led to work with Stevie Van Zandt and then, finally, Bruce and his wife, Patti.

After spending so long just concentrating on how specific strengths and movements were used in competitive sports, it was an amazing chance to see if the things that I taught could be applied in a nonsports situation. And I couldn't have asked for a better—or more challenging—group to work with. These guys had been on the road for just about their whole lives, and the rigors of that lifestyle were taking a toll on their bodies. As they got into their late forties and fifties, it was really forward-thinking of them to realize that they had to make sure that their bodies were in the condition necessary to allow them to continue to do what they loved to do.

It was an incredible assortment of challenges. Clarence Clemons was a huge, six-foot-seven-inch, three-hundred-pound man who had just had his hip replaced. Nils Lofgren, who was maybe five feet two and was a former gymnast and trampoline expert, was also suffering from hip problems. Stevie Van Zandt, the lead guitarist, was as stiff as a corpse and had a world of flexibility issues. And then there was Bruce Springsteen, who's an absolute fanatic about his training and nutrition. Bruce was amazing. At fifty—and now sixty—the guy goes out night after night and performs for three hours while moving constantly. Think about that: he can sing and run at the same time . . . for three hours. Do you have any idea of the kind of conditioning that takes? The next time you're on the treadmill, break into a sprint and try to belt out all five-plus minutes of "Thunder Road."

When the tour ended, I headed back to Florida. Not long after, I got a call from an old friend, Eric Hilcoff, asking me if I'd ever consider working with professional golfers. Jesper Parnevik, a successful, charismatic, and quirky player, was looking for someone to help him out with his strength and conditioning. I'd worked with everyone from pro basketball players to pro baseball players to Rock and Roll Hall of Famers. Golfers? Sure, why not?

GOLFERS ARE ATHLETES . . . AT LEAST SOME OF THEM ARE

It's funny. I come from a football background. I come from a wrestling background. I come from a martial arts background. Obviously, I don't have a problem with intense sports. People see golfers walking around in slacks, polo shirts, and fancy shoes. Books and magazines talk about golf being a "gentleman's game." You always hear about "golf etiquette." I am an in-your-face guy. Just ask any of my players. People that know me are constantly asking me what the heck I'm doing in this sport. They think I should be out on some frozen field in Green Bay or Buffalo working with NFL linebackers, or in some dingy, sweat-filled room right out of *Fight Club* helping some mixed-martial-arts fighter getting ready for his next bout in the Octagon. The last place they picture me is out on some lush fairway somewhere in Hawaii or Arizona hanging out with a bunch of tanned guys dressed in "business casual."

If you had asked me as a kid if I could see myself as a coach in the NFL when I was in my late thirties or early forties, I would have been thrilled with the thought. With my playing days over, it would have been exciting to help younger players make the best of their bodies and abilities in the game. Looking back, though, I think that having had to battle cancer and losing the chance to see if I could make it in the NFL may have made me shy away from football. Maybe because I never got to accomplish a goal I had set for myself, I decided to look elsewhere. I don't want to make it sound as if I'm looking for pity. Anyone that knows me knows that's the last thing I look for. I don't accept a "pity poor me" attitude from my players, so I sure wouldn't accept it from myself. It is what it is, and I think the experience forced me to look for another outlet for my decidedly football mentality.

So how did I end up in golf? Why didn't I just stay on the road with Springsteen? How could a kid from Jersey possibly turn down a chance to live the rock-and-roll life with the Boss?

I got an insider's view of the golf world when I started working with Jesper. I saw a blank canvas. All of the things I knew about the body and biomechanics—and had used to improve athletes in other pro sports—were completely foreign concepts. These things weren't part of the golfer's normal routine. I had the chance to start to dissect the sport, break down the essential movement patterns, and develop things that I knew would work by identifying the way the body needs to work in golf—not as it works in football, not as it works in basketball, but as it works in golf. Once I understood how truly complex the golf movement is, it was easy to begin to teach players how the body has to work—and why it sometimes doesn't work—biomechanically. Just as I did in south Florida, I started to develop a reputation.

Another thing that drew me in was being able to see a side of the sport that most golf fans may not even know exists. A lot of these players have an intensity and a competitive fire that viewers don't see when they watch a tournament on TV. Some guys may say they're just out there playing against the course, but others say that they're going to hit it fifty yards by the other guy all day long. You develop friendships and relationships with other players during the pretty long season, but I don't care if you like someone or not, you don't want him outhitting you by fifty yards on every drive. You don't want him making a birdie every time you shoot par or shoot par every time you make a bogey. What gets lost a lot of the time on TV is that these are competitive individuals. You don't see players trying to distract another player when he's about to tee off. They'll talk, they'll move, they'll stand too close to the guy when he's going through his pre-shot routine. They know all about the so-called etiquette of golf, but they'll do these things just to try to get into the guy's head and mess with him. You don't see this on TV—and you definitely don't get to see (or hear) the expletive-filled threat whipped back at the guy trying to do the distracting. Golf may be a gentleman's game, but these gentlemen know how to drop some serious f-bombs.

A lot of the golfers that were working out with me were guys that were indecisive when growing up about which direction to take their athletic skills. They may have played baseball or basketball in high school—and some of them, such as a Pat Perez or Jason Dufner, had the talent to play, say, pro baseball. But they had to decide about their future. Most of the time they chose golf because of some injury that wouldn't let them play another sport at an elite level.

These guys have always considered themselves athletes. And athletes attract athletes. Think about it. What do most football players, basketball players, and baseball players do in their off-season? They golf. Because of the many celebrity pro-ams, a lot of pros from other sports have befriended pro golfers. This crossover—now more than ever—has reaffirmed to the guys on the tour that they are truly athletes.

That said, not every guy on the tour was going to want—or be able—to work with me. To paraphrase Chris DiMarco, a lot of them just didn't want any part of me. They may be competitive when they're out on the course, but they're the guys I would have beaten up in high school for their lunch money. You have a lot of players that come from money and have spent their whole lives in country clubs. And that's where I saw the challenge. Guys would look at me and tell me they wanted no part of me. I was too aggressive, too intense. I was told by other coaches that when you work with some of these guys on their biomechanics, you have to have a soft touch. You can't be too aggressive. My response? Don't tell me how to do my job. I'm not going to change who I am simply because they weren't used to my approach. Golf is evolving, though, and now they're more accepting of how rigid and demanding I can be because—well—they see the results. I'm not very accepting of someone's saying he can't work out because he's too tired. I'll get on the phone and tell him that he needs to come work with me. Do they like it? Probably not. But I get them in here—whether they're in the mood to work or not—and we do things that make them better as professional golfers.

Of course, then you have someone like Vijay Singh, who grew up in Fiji. He played barefoot as a kid. When I went there with him, it was amazing to see what the sport had done for him. He's beyond famous there. It's surreal. He's on a postage stamp. Everyone—no matter where he goes—knows him and loves him. Here is a guy that, in his late thirties, decided that he was going to change his body to make it able to do everything he needed it to do. Whether it was four in the morning or ten at night, he never gave less than 100 percent when we trained. It was an honor to travel around the world with him and also to see where it all started for him. I'm guessing it is a far cry from where most of today's touring pros got their start.

"Joey D.," he said one time when we were in Fiji, "let's go see the course I grew up playing."

So we get in the car and not only do we drive to the course, we drive right onto the course. I was like "Vij, what are you doing?" and he calmly says it's okay to drive on the course. It was mind-blowing. Imagine driving a car onto the most pristine fairway or green at Pebble Beach or Augusta National. Of course, the holes he grew up playing weren't quite as manicured as those on the PGA Tour. You could barely tell where the fairway started or ended or where the green was. Parking, though, wasn't much of a problem.

TODAY

I don't care what you do for a living, if someone can make you better at whatever you do—can improve you to the point where you're more successful and earning more money—you do it. It's a no-brainer. I'm giving you information that if you use it and apply it, it's only going to help you to stay injury-free, to discover your weaknesses and overcome them, and to take your strengths and make them more effective. You put all of these things together, and when you step up to the first tee, you have such confidence because you know you've worked on things again and again and again with this insane guy who doesn't really look like your normal golf-biomechanics coach.

My job is to bridge the gap between the Old World Golfer and the New World Golfer. But it's getting easier; even on the Champions Tour (formerly the Seniors Tour), you have Kent Bigglestaff working with guys in their fifties and older. Twenty years ago, you had guys that wouldn't even have considered going to a gym. After a round, they'd head straight to the bar. There's still a touch of that. Some guys will come into our trailer and look around as if they'd just landed on a foreign planet. "Is this where I get a rubdown?" they'll ask. I'll look at them and say, "No. This is the trailer for athletes. It's where work gets done. It's where biomechanics are assessed and worked on, and where core strength, coordination, and cardiovascular endurance are improved." Okay, maybe I don't say it that nicely.

What's so exciting about golf-specific training and conditioning is the level of acceptance it's achieved. By the time that Vijay and I decided to go our separate ways in 2007, the biomechanical approach that we had taken was no longer looked upon as crazy or outlandish. I'm no longer the nut running on the beach playing a game of "medicine-ball catch" with a touring pro. Now I'm the nut teaching about biomechanics and the science of movement at the PGA Tour Academy at TPC Sawgrass—the St. Andrew's of America. I'm working with more than a dozen touring pros who, week after week, are still vying for the top money late into Sunday afternoon. I'm working with some of the top junior golfers in the country to help them understand the science behind what it's going to take to be successful at the high school, collegiate, and—eventually—pro level. And I have a wonderful working arrangement with Greg Hopkins and the people at Cleveland Golf.

Maybe even more thrilling, though, is that these tools and teachings can be used by anyone. Age isn't a limitation. Experience isn't a limitation. Equipment isn't a limitation. I don't care if you're a touring pro or a recreational player with a thirty handicap. Golf is just a series of biomechanical movements, and we are all bound by the laws of physics. To achieve the results you want, you have to be able to do certain things with your body. Only by making the necessary changes in your body will you have the ability to master the complexities of the golf swing and be able to play the game better and enjoy it more. My program was developed—and used successfully—by the top players in the world, but it isn't just for pros. This is for everyone. This is for the world of golf.

What Is Biomechanics?

or . . . Creating Movement, Not Chaos

Biomechanics can be described as the study of how forces exerted both internally (by the muscles) and externally (by gravity) affect the skeletal system. That's a pretty heady and dry statement, and I'm sure plenty of you nodded off to dreamland when you heard a line like that in a college lecture. I'll go into the science in a little bit, but let me try to explain things in a little more easy-to-wrap-your-brain-around way.

The golf swing is essentially about two things. You create movement, then you control movement. The movement that you create starts with your takeaway and must be controlled all the way up to the top of your backswing, then down through impact and follow-through. The best golfers create and control their movements perfectly.

If you don't understand from a biomechanical viewpoint what has to happen in a golf swing, and if your body isn't capable of doing these things, then you're doomed to a continuous cycle of creating—and then trying to control—chaos. You slice the ball, you hook the ball, you lack accuracy and power, and, eventually, it all falls apart.

You need to create and control movement, not chaos.

I, ROBOT

Before we can even talk about creating and controlling movement, we have to go over the basics of how the body moves. To truly understand how that happens, we need to talk about robots. Let's take the *bio* off *biomechanics* for a second and

I can explain—in a purely mechanical way—how our bones, muscles, tendons, etc., let us do all of the things that we do.

Picture yourself as a giant robot—a mechanical man or woman—made up of a metal-framework "skeleton." From a standing position, if you want to raise your hand to touch your shoulder by bending at the elbow, you'd need some sort of cable system attached at both the shoulder and the elbow on the front of the arm that could be cranked to pull the forearm upward until the fingertips of your hand touched the front of your shoulder. The cable system is your muscles. In this case, the muscle would be your biceps. The chains at the very ends of the cable that connect the cable to the metal skeleton are your tendons. The forearm gets raised because the cranking of the cable system causes the slack cable to tighten and shorten. This shortening of the cable (or muscle) causes—actually forces—the forearm to move.

Most of the muscles that let you move a certain way are complemented by other muscles that allow you to move in the opposite way.

Muscles grow by being exposed to greater and greater resistances. It doesn't take much strength to lift your fingertips to your shoulder by flexing your elbow. If you wanted to lift a one-gallon bottle to your shoulder by bending at the elbow, though, you'd need to generate more pulling force to be able to lift your forearm. The robot version of you would need a stronger—or larger—cable system. You, though, would need stronger biceps. This—in about half a dozen sentences—is how strength training works. It's not all that difficult to understand. You get bigger and stronger by doing things that require you to be bigger and stronger.

This is a basic version of how our bones, muscles, and tendons play and grow together. The elbow is a simple joint. It's a hinge. For the most part, it can only move one way. From the same standing position as before, you can't, for example, bend the elbow in the opposite direction so that the back of your hand touches the back of your shoulder. If by chance your elbow did bend that way, it would be accompanied by an ear-piercing scream by you.

The mechanics of movement at the elbow are easy to understand, and movement at the elbow is easy to control. It's why you rarely miss your mouth with your fork.

Things get a lot more complicated when you look at the shoulders. Unlike the simple hinge of the elbow, the shoulder is a ball-and-socket joint. Think of all of the ways you can move your entire arm—directly in front of you like a sleepwalker, out to the sides like a guy trying to make his body look like the letter *T*, straight up in the air as you did when you sank that twenty-six-foot putt, etc. In addition, muscles at the shoulder allow you to rotate your arm.

With your arms extended directly in front of you, you can rotate your arms so that your palms are facing up, then rotate them so that your palms are facing down. To do all of this, you need a whole mess of cable systems and plenty of chains to attach those cables to the metal framework. Motion around the shoulder is a lot harder to control than motion around the elbow. You may never miss your mouth when eating with a fork. You can bend your elbow to the same degree and at the same speed and intensity repeatedly without really thinking about it. But what if you had to eat by tossing your food way up in the air underhand and catching it in your mouth? You'd end up doing a lot more laundry. And you'd probably be a few pounds lighter.

Now, think about the golf swing. It involves just about every muscle and movement around every joint in the body. In addition to movement at the shoulders and elbows, you have—among other things—movement (and rotation) at the wrist, rotation of the spine, an insane amount of action around the hips, as well as movement at the knees, ankles, and even the balls of your feet. With this many moving parts that need to be controlled in, literally, the blink of an eye, there's no shortage of ways that chaos can be created.

Biomechanically, it would seem, humans are about as predisposed to playing golf as hamsters are to going scuba diving. The human body is an incredible thing, though. The interaction between the nervous system (the brain, spinal cord, and the network of nerves that run through the body), the skeletal system (the bones and the ligaments that connect them together), and the muscular system (the muscles and the tendons that connect them to the bones) allow our bodies to adapt to just about anything. Thanks to the communication and cooperation among these systems, you can build stronger and more powerful muscles, recover from any number of injuries, and learn complex movements such as riding a bicycle or juggling three tennis balls. When all three systems are properly conditioned, you can even learn how to perform a really sweet golf swing.

THE GOLF SWING

Now that you have a sense of how the human body moves, I want to break down the golf swing, so you'll see what has to happen every time you swing a club. It'll give you an idea of the theories and philosophies that I work with. I'm not going to tell you what you should be doing to hit the ball longer or harder—that's the job of a swing coach or the pro at your club. All I'm telling you is what your body has to go through to get the ball from point A to point B in proper golf fashion.

When you step up to the first tee, the first thing you do is to try to find your body's center or where your balance point is. Sometimes you'll hear it referred to as the waggle. Sergio Garcia was famous for having twenty-three waggles—almost two dozen mini-swings that let him find his balance. I don't recommend you go through the same lengthy pre-shot routine. Your friends will stop wanting to play with you, and if you ever do make it to the big time, you'll bore TV viewers to tears. I do recommend, though, that you do whatever it takes—within reason—to help you get centered and balanced at address. Again, there's a whole lot of movement and moving parts during the swing, and even if everything else is done perfectly, if you start from an out-of-balance position, you're going to be creating chaos.

Why do some people have better balance than other people? First of all, and perhaps most frustrating to admit, some people are just born with better balance. It makes sense. Some people are just born with abilities—ridiculous flexibility, amazing agility, whippetlike speed—that gives them an edge on their peers. Second, and more important, balance is one of those abilities— just like flexibility, agility, and speed—that can be improved by working on it. You get more flexible by working on your flexibility. You improve your balance by working on your balance. Most people assume that because they had lousy balance as a kid and could never walk the balance beam in elementary-school gym class, they are doomed to a life of bumbling awkwardness. You may never be able to quit your job to become a tightrope walker in the circus, but balance can easily be improved in just about anyone—and these improvements will show up almost immediately in your golf game.

So, now you've found your center. It's the calm before the storm. Nothing is moving. You're comfortable with your posture and spine angle. You're aware of your body's position from your shoulders down to your waist, from your waist to your hips, from your hips to your knees, and from your knees to your ankles. Your arms are extended and you've waggled yourself into a comfortable and confident position with your club.

Let's hit the "pause" button for a second. How's your posture when you're sitting at your desk or behind the wheel of your car? How's your posture when you're waiting at the bank or at your favorite coffee place? Are your back and shoulders sloped and rounded forward? Think about this: if you're already forward-pitched when you're trying to stand or sit up straight, imagine how out-of-whack curled-forward you are when you lean into golf posture. Poor posture translates into an inconsistent spine angle that prevents you from ever getting a true and perfect rotation in either your takeaway and backswing or downswing and follow-through. If ideal rotation in the golf swing could be compared to screwing a perfectly straight screw into a piece of wood, swinging a golf club with poor posture would be as awkward, ugly, and unpredictable as trying to screw a bent screw into a piece of wood. Happily, it's easy to improve your posture by strengthening the specific muscles that keep you upright.

And now back to our golf swing.

Here comes the fun part—the moment when you can either create movement or chaos. All of a sudden, the golf swing starts. Like a dragster, you burst into action. During takeaway, your club head travels between forty and fifty miles per hour as you take it up to the top of your backswing. Unlike a dragster, though, which uses a chute to help it stop, you only have your body to stop this 50 mph movement. Your body has to not only stop the club from moving at the top of the backswing, but also slingshot the clubhead back in the opposite direction as you begin your downswing.

People don't generally think of golf as a sport that requires much strength, but do you realize the amount of force being applied to the muscles of the hips, shoulders, and chest, as well as the muscles that rotate the spine at the top of the backswing? If you're not strong enough to stop the momentum that you began at takeaway, you're in trouble. In a best-case scenario, you're going to take yourself out of position and end up swinging blindly at your ball. In a worst-case scenario, you're going to lack the stability and balance to keep yourself upright and end up falling backward. I've been around for a while and I know that neither of these things will earn you your tour card.

"Wait," you might say. "If my takeaway and backswing involve such Herculean feats of strength, balance, and stability, why can't I just start my whole swing at the top of my backswing?"

You could—if you didn't mind losing a giant chunk of your power and adding a dozen or so strokes to every round you played. Who knows? Maybe our earliest golfing ancestors out on some field in Scotland a few hundred years ago played this way. You do have a lot more control over your swing. My guess, though, is that it ended the first time Angus's bigger and stronger golfing buddy outdrove him on the first eight holes and then announced—in a deep Scottish brogue—"I'm gonna hit it fifty by you all day long." A seething Angus, of course, grabbed his primitive dogwood-headed club, lined up his ball, reared back, and uncorked a shot that probably changed the game forever. It's this takeaway into the backswing that gives you the extra power that leads to greater distances. Think of it this way. Imagine stepping up to your ball, addressing it with perfect spine angle and golf posture, drawing your driver back, say, a foot and a half, then swinging. I don't care if you have the most beautiful, make-the-angels-cry swing in the history of the game, the ball's going to travel about as far as it would have if you'd hit it with your pitching wedge.

The farther you can get the clubhead to travel, the more momentum it can build up. This leads to more speed and more power at impact. And this leads to greater distances. Those extra few degrees of rotation that you get by taking your club dynamically back to the top of your backswing are what allow your clubhead to travel farther during your swing. But while a powerful backswing can lead to greater distances, it also can lead to greater problems.

Again, you have to be able to stop yourself at the top of the backswing. You have to stop this freight train of a movement, bring it to dead stop, then—without losing your spine angle—rotate your body back around toward the ball with your clubhead reaching speeds that exceed 100 mph. At impact, your entire body—everything from your fingers maintaining the proper grip on your club down to your toes properly moving to guarantee a perfect pivot at the ball of your foot—must be on the same page to make sure that you are striking the ball at maximum speed and with proper clubface angle.

It's a daunting task, but guess what? You're not done yet!

You somehow have to stop this locomotive that's now traveling more than 100 mph. If you thought it was tough to stop your 50 mph takeaway at the top of your backswing, it can be even tougher to stop your 100-plus mph follow-through.

That's it. Pretty simple, huh? And, oh, yeah, you have to do that with proper speed and intensity using various-length clubs somewhere between 50 and, heck, 150 times every round—depending on how good you are. Let's face it, everyone's made a shot that he would describe as perfect. Perfect distance, perfect height, perfect bounce, perfect spin, perfect everything. It makes for great postround barroom talk. Sadly, for most golfers, these shots are the exception and not the rule. While you may chalk up your killer drive or dead-on approach shot to your skills, the odds are it was more luck than anything else. If you hit the ball enough times, it's eventually going to do exactly what you want it to do. It's just a variation on the "infinite monkeys" theory. Give an infinite number of monkeys an infinite number of typewriters, and eventually one of them is going to bang out *Romeo and Juliet*. You need to make the perfect shot the rule and not the exception. You need to lessen the role of luck by upping your body's ability to perform optimally. Golf, at the top levels, is about being able to re-create that perfect shot every time.

And that brings us back to robots. . . .

IRON BYRON

In the midsixties, shaft maker True Temper developed a machine that would help it test and compare the performances of its various products. This pneumatically powered robot would allow the manufacturer to see how its existing and prototype shafts held up in an incredibly controlled environment. The robot—eventually nicknamed Iron Byron because its swing eerily mimicked that of golfing legend Byron Nelson—was programmed to strike the ball with the same 109 mph clubhead speed at impact every time. Product testing before that had been done by human golfers and was far less exact. Even if you had the same guy, with essentially the same swing, hitting ball after ball to test the merits of such and such new shaft, some consistency would be lost somewhere. The swing might look the same, but no one is going to execute their nine-hundredth drive exactly the same as their one-hundredth drive. Unless, of course, that guy is a machine.

In 1974, the United States Golf Association, the governing body of the sport, adopted Iron Byron as its means of testing balls. Today, the USGA still uses a golfing robot to test equipment, but the current Byron is a more modern, electrically powered machine.

I don't expect your swing to become as replicable as Byron's. He's just a series of fixed parts designed solely to hit golf balls. That's all he can do. He can't play badminton, take out the trash, do jumping jacks, etc. You, on the other hand, can do all of these things and more. Mechanically, you're capable of doing far more things than Iron Byron.

When designing the original Byron, though, engineers struggled with exactly the same issues that you and I are dealing with now. They had to figure out how to get his swing arm to come back far enough to create the necessary clubhead speed at impact. They had to figure out how bottom-heavy and stable the unit had to be so it wouldn't be thrown off-balance during the swing. I could go on. Fortunately for them, they could correct their golfer's "body" with the turn of a screw, the sliding and readjusting of a metal arm, or through the use of any number of things from a toolbox full of toys. Correcting the human golfer is a little more involved. Even though I've been tempted to go after a player or two of mine with a screwdriver or a wrench, I know that the only way to transform the body into a finely tuned "golf machine" is through personalized and golf-specific training.

GOLF-SPECIFIC TRAINING

Again, my point is that the golf swing is one of the most complex movements in all of sports. To turn yourself into a living, breathing version of Iron Byron and be able to—time after time—hit the ball perfectly, you need to fix your body so it can do what it has to do with the club. Once that happens, you're free to concentrate on the things that the pro at your club is telling you to do. You no longer have to worry about your body's infrastructure and can concentrate on how to use—and rely on—your body's muscles and joints to let you play the way you want. It's an incredibly liberating feeling that will help you play better and enjoy the game more. Imagine if every morning when you left your house, you not only had to focus on the meetings and presentations that you had that day at the office, but you also had to worry if the wind was going to blow the shutters off your windows while you were gone or if your garage door was going to cave in before you got home. That's the kind of mental confusion that most golfers carry onto the course. They not only have to focus on all of the things that their pro told them, they also have to worry about their bodies being able to follow through on those things. Properly training your body can clear up that mental confusion. You're free to create and control movement, not chaos.

That means training your body specifically to do the things it needs to do. Your lower body has to be able to maintain its balance and stability while your upper body goes through a series of dynamic and extreme rotations. A certain amount of separation is needed between your upper and lower body to allow you to rotate sufficiently in both your backswing and follow-through. The range of motion around your shoulder joints has to be adequate to let you take the club comfortably through the entire swing. But even if all of these body parts are individually prepared to do what they need to do, you still need to have the overall body awareness to make sure that things happen—and muscles come into play—when they're supposed to happen.

Training your body to make it as strong as it can be—from a biomechanical perspective—for golf means working on a lot of muscles and body parts that you probably never thought to work on. Heck, you're going to be working on muscles that you've probably never even heard of. And the muscles that you have heard of need to be strengthened in ways you may not even have considered.

As a quick example, let's look at the major muscle that makes up the chest, the pectoralis major. A traditional exercise program works the chest by having you do bench presses. During a standard bench press, you're lying on your back on a bench and pushing a barbell or a pair of dumbbells away from you toward the ceiling. The movement is completely linear. You move the weight from point A to point B and back again. The golf swing isn't linear. A pushing movement isn't really required during the golf swing. Your chest muscles mainly come into play at the top of your backswing. They are part of the stability-and-braking system that allows you to stop your club and slingshot it back into your downswing. Your pecs, therefore, not only need to be strong enough to be able to do this, they must be loose enough to let you get your arms in the position they need to be. If your pecs are too tight, there's no way you can get your arms back far enough. If the arms can't get to where they need to be, your club can't get to where it needs to be. If you can't get your club back far enough, you won't be able to get the rotation necessary to generate the velocity and clubhead speed that you need at impact. The result is less distance on your shot. So, while a traditional weight-training regimen may make your pecs stronger, it can also make your pecs overly tight. A golf-specific regimen—such as the one here—will make sure that the muscles are strong enough *and* loose enough to get the job done.

Once you understand the biomechanics of the golf swing, you'll understand why this book is different from just about every other golf or fitness book out there. I'm not here to tell you how to perform the perfect swing; I'm here to show you what's currently preventing you from ever being able to perform that perfect swing. By using the same assessments that I use with my players, you'll discover your body's limitations in certain areas—whether it be flexibility, strength, balance, or overall coordination. Once you know what's holding you back, you're going to have the tools to fix those problems—not through generic, cookie-cutter muscle-magazine workouts, but through golf-specific exercises designed to treat your individual issues.

3 Biomechanics and the Golf Pro

or . . . Don't Just Take My Word for It

Of course I want to sell you on the merits of taking a biomechanical approach to improving your golf game. I understand the concepts behind such phrases as "Fix your body, fix your swing" and "Create movement, not chaos." I know that the programs I design for players work. My track record with some of the top golfers speaks for itself. But I'm a biomechanics coach, so, of course I'm going to try to convince you of the importance of biomechanics. If I were an exterminator, it'd be my job to tell you that your house needs to be sprayed, and if I were a baker, it'd be my job to tell you that you need to eat more pie.

So let's get a second opinion. Let's talk to a teaching professional to get a view from another side of the golf world to see how biomechanical assessment and training fits in with more traditional golf teaching. Todd Jones is the head instructor at the PGA Tour Academy at TPC Sawgrass in Ponte Vedra, Florida. You don't end up in that position by accident. He knows the golf swing better than just about anyone else out there.

Todd says:

As recently as ten years ago, I'd find myself working with a player on his golf swing and we'd discover that we just weren't able to make the changes that, in an ideal world, we'd like to be able to make. The player's body couldn't do it. It would become frustrating for both the teacher and the student. We'd be able to do things in slow motion and force the body into the position it needed to be in, but when the player got out on the golf course and then added speed into the equation, he couldn't physically repeat what we'd been able to do in slow motion. The improvements we'd made weren't being transferred onto the golf course.

Back around 2002, I started to take a look at why some of my students weren't getting any better. That led me to really take a look at what their bodies could and couldn't do. To be able to blend my teaching with what Joey does has just been amazing. He not only has the knowledge of the body and biomechanics, but he also understands the golf swing very well.

There are individuals whom I've worked with for a while and have finally been able to convince that a biomechanical approach is the way to go. When we get into that initial evaluation and assessment, everyone has a smile on their face, because we start to see what their bodies can—and cannot—do. From there, it's easy to trace things back and say, "Aha! That's why we're struggling in this or that area of swing mechanics." In an ideal world, everyone I work with would also be working with Joey. He paves the way for what I can do. He paves the way so that there is range of motion, so that when we start working on concepts, not only can we achieve them in slow motion, we can take them to the golf course.

Take a look at the generation that's on the Champions Tour right now. They didn't grow up with an understanding of the body or coaches that understood the body. Many of them played with or played around physical restrictions, which dictated certain things to happen in their golf swing that might not have been mechanically efficient. Now we have a choice. We can partner with a biomechanics coach and start working on changing the body, or we can say to the player, "Your body is what it is. Let's go work on your short game."

Your typical recreational player has restrictions that need to be addressed regularly. If we can get those addressed, it allows the player to improve quickly and dramatically. Most recreational players have issues with their rotator cuffs. They lack the range of motion and the strength in the rotator cuff to swing the golf club on plane. People don't go into their gym or fitness facility and say, "I'm going to train my rotator cuffs today." You just don't hear that. No one says, "I'm going to stretch out my rotator cuffs." But every day when he's on tour, Joey is working on rotator-cuff flexibility and rotator-cuff strength with guys in the trailer, as well as on range-of-motion exercises involving the hips and hamstrings and lower back.

Golf, in itself, doesn't build any significant level of strength or flexibility, but it takes a tremendous amount of both to be able to consistently control a clubhead that's traveling upward of 120 mph at impact. Because of this, a golfer needs to train as aggressively as he would train if he were playing any other sport. Anyone looking to improve has to look at it that way.

The neat thing about Joey's approach is that it's not only a process of gaining flexibility and strength. It's also a process of gaining awareness and being able to control the moving parts of the body. This is important, because another major problem that most players have is balance. We know that once a person is off-balance, all bets are off. That's because their subconscious sense of equilibrium kicks in, and they're not worried about striking a little white object anymore. They're worried, subconsciously, about staying upright. To compensate for this lack of balance and stability, the swing becomes dominated by the upper body, the arms, and the hands. And that's not an efficient way to transfer energy through impact. Proper training can make an individual more mechanically sound throughout more of the swing. If an individual is mechanically sound in the fundamental positions—above and beyond simply address—he's going to be able to repeat his swing through impact position consistently.

The training routines that improve biomechanics are actually practice routines improving the game. Once you start to educate students to that fact, they realize that they can take a half hour and walk through a training program that's actually as good as a half hour of practice. They've been going over golf-specific range-of-motion exercises and golf-specific drills that are designed to carry over onto the golf course. It can also carry over into other places. It's exciting to see what happens when someone really wants to make a change. Not only is it a change for their game, but often it's a change for their lifestyle. It's getting healthy for golf and getting healthy for life at the same time.

I see Joey's work as being integral to the growth and future of the game in a couple of ways. First off, the average golf score hasn't dropped that much in the past, say, ten years. As things such as time and money come at more and more of a premium, people aren't going to continue to dedicate themselves to something that frustrates them. As much as you may love the pursuit of a better score, it can be frustrating if you're trying to improve and you're not improving. Using techniques that change the body is a way for players to exceed their expectations, because we know that if the body is prepared to do things, it's not difficult to change a motor skill.

I also see the biomechanics approach emerging strongly with my generation of teaching professionals and swing coaches. In ten years, ideally, each teaching professional will be teaching with a biomechanics coach. Through their relationship, the golf professional will know enough about biomechanics to understand where a player's limitations may be and can get the biomechanics coach involved right away.

As you can see, Todd understands how biomechanics goes hand in hand with what he does and how well it complements working with a pro or a swing coach. We'll be hearing more from Todd later on. Now it's time to actually get to work.

How to Use This Book

---

or . . . Here Are the Rules

If you've made it this far, it shows me you're serious about changing your body so that you can change your swing. Consider yourself lucky: all you had to do was make it through a couple of chapters about me and about the science of biomechanics. My players show me that they're serious about changing their game by getting up at four in the morning to work out with me. Whatever the case—whether you're a tour professional wiping the sleep out of his eyes or a weekend player who just read my life story—you're about to get busy.

What I love about this program, and what makes it so effective, is that it's specific to golf and it's specific to you. Again, it's not a generic full-body strength and conditioning workout. A workout like that is great, and if you do it correctly, it'll help you to look and feel better. As you've probably been able to figure out, I'm a giant fan of fitness. The fitter you are, the better your quality of life is going to be. This book, though, is about getting your body in the shape it needs to be in to play golf—not tennis, not basketball, not yoga, not mixed martial arts.

I'm not here to have you do dead lifts, power cleans, or squats. This is a completely different planet. Even if you've spent your life in the gym, I'm going to be having you doing things you've never done before. I don't care if you can squat three times your weight. That's all well and good, and I'm sure it impresses the hell out of the guys at the gym, but it's not what golf is about. I'm here to get you to be able to, say, move your pelvis two inches. What I do is not "personal training." I may end up using an exercise similar to what the trainer in your gym may have a client do, but when I do, it's a variation of the movement that makes it golf-specific.

THE RULES—PART ONE

The program is broken down into two sections. First is the assessments and prescriptions section. Here, you'll go through a series of six assessments that will tell you exactly where your body is too tight, not quite strong enough, out of balance, etc. These are the things that are preventing you from being able to play your best. They are the things that are keeping your body from being the finely tuned instrument that it needs to be. Again, and I'm going to say this about a million times, you need to fix your body before you can fix your swing.

Once you've gone through the assessments, it's time to go to the prescriptions. Here you'll find specific exercises that you need to do to correct whatever problems or limitations were revealed in the assessments. Don't worry, I'm not going to give you dozens of rehab exercises. Each assessment has only three or four corrective exercises. You're busy. I'm busy. I don't want you spending all day in the gym or at home working out. I want you out enjoying the best golf you've ever played. You're going to be amazed by how much impact a few simple exercises will have on your body and your game. The three or four corrective movements that I may have you doing will let you fix your body without forcing you to give up much of your time.

In addition to giving you the specifics on how—and why—you're doing the exercises, I'll also fill you in on the science behind what you're doing. Golfers are smart people, so I figured you'd want to know some of the biology and physics behind what the exercises accomplish. I'll tell you what muscles are involved in the various movements and what their roles are in your golf game. You're going to develop some serious appreciation for some of the smaller muscles in the hips, core, and shoulders—muscles you've probably never even heard of before.

I'm also going to tell you what you're probably experiencing out on the course as a result of your specific limitations. I may come across as a psychic or like some sort of "Sherlock Holmes of golf" when I tell you that if you're a right-handed golfer with limited external rotation around the shoulder, you're probably slicing the ball a lot. All I'm doing, though, is reading your body. If you have limited external shoulder rotation on the side of your takeaway, I know you're going to slice the ball. If you show up at my place with sour cream, salsa, and guacamole on your shirt, I know you had Mexican food for lunch. It's no different. Ideally we get to the point where if I read your body, I'd determine that, biomechanically, you have the potential to be a damn good golfer.

THE RULES—PART TWO

Once you've determined which exercises you need to do to correct whatever limitations your body has, it's time to head into the second section of the program—the Joey D. Dozen. Everyone who uses the book should do these twelve exercises. They'll help you to strengthen what needs to be strengthened, lengthen what needs to be lengthened, and, generally, let you fine-tune your golf body. Even if you passed every assessment (which few people—pros included—will do), you should be doing this workout. It won't help your tennis game, your surfing, or your kayaking, but it will improve your body's biomechanical ability to do what it needs to do when swinging a golf club.

In chapter 13 I'll give you a detailed plan on how to fit all of these exercises into your schedule. I don't expect you to become a gym rat. Ideally, you're able to commit to three twenty-minute workouts a week. That's just an hour a week that is going to powerfully impact your golf game. Think it's going to be tough to squeeze an hour of work into your already busy schedule? Heck, I bet if you added it up, you spend at least an hour every week just *worrying* about your golf game. Replace that worry with an hour of personalized and golf-specific training designed to alleviate that worrying and you're good to go.

Don't get discouraged if the assessments show you that you have a lot of work to do. Again, it's not going to add up to hours in the gym. In those same twenty minutes, I'll make sure that you're doing something to address all of the issues identified in your assessments. You'll do a few things from the Joey D. Dozen and a few things from the prescriptions department. If anything, breaking it down that way is going to keep the program more varied and more exciting for you. The main reason that people abandon a fitness program is boredom. Every workout is the same. It's a drag. That won't happen here. Because you'll rarely be doing more than eight or nine different exercises per workout—and overall, you may need to do over forty different exercises—you may never end up doing the same workout twice.

THE RULES—PART THREE

My only request when you do the assessments is that you're 100 percent honest with yourself. Golfers are the greatest compensators in the world. If an assessment checks to see if you can, say, rotate your body a certain amount without your knee turning in, that's what I want you to check. Period. End of statement. I'm not asking to see how far you can rotate with your knee turning in "just a little bit," "a smidgen," or "a hair." That's not the way it works. You won't get the most out of my program if you're not honest with yourself. Even worse, your golf buddies—who know that you're reading my book—will think

> Before, I would tend to slack off. When I didn't feel like working out, I usually didn't. But ever since I've been with Joey, he motivates me. Even if I'm not feeling great, he'll pull me into the trailer and say, "You need to do this. You need to that. Otherwise, I'm going to beat you down." So I listen to him.
> —*Ryuji Imada,*
> *touring professional*

> I'm always letting him know that he needs to relax. We're not in the mixed-martial-arts world. You can't just go crack somebody's head open because they did something. I'm trying to get him to not be so serious about everything. I don't know if it's working or not.
> —*Jason Dufner,*
> *touring professional*

that I don't know what I'm talking about. If you use this book correctly, you will improve your game. I guarantee it. Use it wrong, though, and we'll all look bad. I'm not into looking bad. And ask any of my players—I'm far more fun to be around when I'm in a good mood.

THE RULES—PART FOUR

Just as it says on the shampoo bottle: "Apply, rinse, repeat." To chart your progress and see how much the exercises in both the Joey D. Dozen and the prescription sections are improving your ability to move your body, I want you to assess yourself every three months. It's not too much to ask. You change the oil in your car every three months to make sure it's running optimally. Assessing your range of motion to make sure that your body continues to approach its optimal condition shouldn't be too much to ask. And you're not just checking the assessments that you may have had trouble with—you're going to go through all six of them. What you'll probably find is that even the ones that you may have earned a "passing" mark on initially are now even easier to do. It's a good feeling.

The program you're about to begin is the same one used by many of the top golfers in the world—the guys that are still playing for the top money on Sunday afternoon. The program will show you exactly what your body's biomechanical limitations are. It will then give you what you need to address those issues and help you learn how to work your entire body to make it as structurally sound as it can be for the sport of golf. I've done my part—I've given you everything that you need to do to improve your game. Now it's your turn.

Enjoy the journey.

5 Biomechanical Assessments

or . . . Why You Bought This Book

When I start working with a player, the first thing I do is to put him or her through a series of assessments. This lets me know where the player stands in terms of range of motion, strength, rotation, etc. These are not arbitrary assessments. These are specific tests to see where a player may have issues that will—from a biomechanical standpoint—prevent him from swinging a club as well as he can. This series of assessments is a golf-centric way to see exactly what a player's body is capable of—and not capable of. Once we learn where a player has issues, it's time to fix the body, so we can fix the swing.

You're about to go through the same series of assessments.

The only way that these assessments are going to mean anything is if you are 100 percent truthful. This isn't a multiple-choice exam. I do not want you to send me a five-hundred-word essay for each assessment. These are simple yes or no questions. If I asked you whether the sky was blue, I would expect you to tell me—based on the time of day and the weather—either yes or no. I wouldn't expect you to tell me that the color blue makes you sad or want to read a poem you'd written about falling in love under a brilliant blue sky. The things that I'm asking you about are straight facts: can you do such and such?

For each assessment, your yes or no answer will tell you what you need to do to fix your body. If you're unable to perform all the movements correctly in the first assessment, which checks shoulder rotation, for example, you'll need to add the prescription exercises for that assessment to your workout. You'll find those exercises in chapter 6. If you're able to perform all of the movements required of you in the assessment, you won't have to add the prescription exercises to your workout. By focusing on the specifics of your own, unique, one-of-a-kind body, these assessments will help you come up with a program that targets exactly what needs to be targeted. It becomes a laser beam of a workout that hones in on your particular issues without forcing you to do a lot of time-consuming exercises that you may not need.

I'll go into some of the science and reasoning behind the assessments while you do them. When you get to the prescription chapters for the particular assessments, I'll give you a deeper insight into the scientific, biomechanical, and golf-specific aspects of each exercise. If you pass an assessment and don't need to go the prescription chapter, I still want you to have an idea of why it's important to have, say, sufficient range of motion around the shoulder and the ability to externally rotate it to a certain point. Of course, even if you pass an assessment, feel free to read the prescription chapter anyway. You may not have to do any of the exercises, but you may want to learn more about what makes up the optimal golfer's body.

I don't believe in using a lot of fancy equipment. When I'm on the road and at tournaments with my players, we do just about all of our work in the trailer. And as you're going to see from the pictures, there's not a whole lot of room in there—especially when you have a few guys working out at the same time. For the actual workouts, you're going to need some resistance bands. I suggest Golf-Gym PowerBandz—they were specially designed by me for golfers and I believe that they're the top bands on the market for golf-specific training. They're what I use with my players. In fact, just about every pro who works out in the trailer uses them, whether they're one of my players or not. That's a pretty strong endorsement. And I take it as a compliment on my equipment-designing skills.

Other than the bands, the only things you'll need to track down for both the assessments and the workouts are:

A stability ball. I would go with a sixty-five-centimeter ball.
An eight-pound medicine ball. If you want to get one with handles, that's fine.
A pair of light dumbbells. And I mean light dumbbells. Five pounds.
A golf club. You probably have one kicking around.

Go to my Web site at www.golfgym.com if you need to get any of this equipment. Check out the appendix at the end of the book for a special offer.

Everything else you need is right where you left it:

Your body.
Gravity.

Before you begin, I want you to take a few minutes to get your body warm and loose. If you have access to a treadmill or an elliptical machine, hop onto it and work it for three or four minutes. If you don't have access to a machine, no problem. You can walk or jog in place or do jumping jacks for a few minutes. The idea is to get your body warm.

After your warm-up, your heart should be beating a little bit faster than normal and you may have broken a slight sweat. Your body is about to be tested. Don't worry—this isn't going to be the only time you do these assessments. Remember, you're going to be doing them every three months. That way, you can not only

> The golf club does not move on its own. You can't set it up against the desk, say, "Move," to it, and have it move. It moves because your body moves it. I see the individual that takes advantage of a complete training program accelerating quickly through the improvement process, because not only are they going to be working on the proper drills for golf-swing mechanics, they're making sure that their body can move through the necessary range of motion.
>
> —Todd Jones, Head Instructor, PGA Tour Academy

be sure that the program that you're on is tailored specifically to your body's needs, but you can track the progress that you're making. My guess, though, is that you'll be feeling and experiencing that progress on the golf course before you even get a chance to do a second set of assessments.

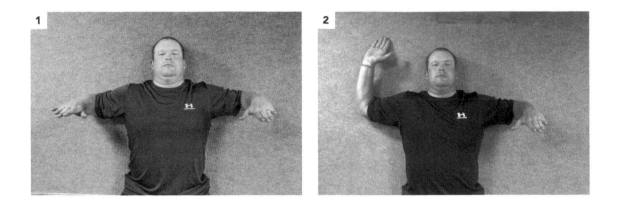

ASSESSMENT ONE—SHOULDER ROTATION

Back in the chapter on biomechanics, I told you about the importance of the backswing. Your ability to get the clubhead back a few extra degrees will let you generate more power and clubhead speed through your downswing and through impact. I also talked about how important it was to be able to control and stop your club during your follow-through. If you've got limited rotation around the shoulder, that limitation will affect both of these abilities.

I see players of all skill levels having trouble with tightness in the shoulders. This assessment will let you know how well your shoulders rotate.

How to do it   Stand with your back against a wall and your feet about shoulders' width apart. Raise your upper arms up so that they're parallel to the ground with the backs of your arms pressed against the wall. Your forearms should be aimed forward—also parallel to the floor—with your palms facing down. This is the starting position. See Jason Gore in Picture One.

Slowly—and without moving any other parts of your body—rotate your right forearm up and try to see if you can get the back of your right forearm and the back of your right hand to touch the wall. Your forearm should be perpendicular to the floor and your elbow should be flexed at exactly ninety degrees. Ideally, you should look as if you are testifying in court. See Picture Two.

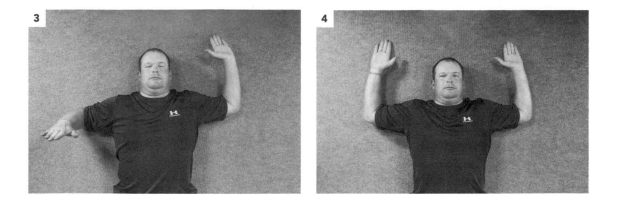

Having sufficient range of motion and external rotation at the shoulder means that you're able to touch the wall with your forearm and the back of your hand without your elbow dropping or coming away from the wall or your back arching. If either of these things are happening—or if you're experiencing pain trying to do this—you have some shoulder-rotation issues.

Return to the starting position and now attempt the same move by rotating your left forearm up toward the wall. Again, look for the same results—and also look for the compensations that I mentioned above (elbow dropping, elbow coming away from the wall, your back arching). See Picture Three.

Finally, return to the starting position and attempt the move with both arms simultaneously. Try to get the backs of both forearms and the backs of both hands to touch the wall without any of the compensations occurring. See Picture Four.

How'd it go? If you weren't able to get both of your hands individually—and then together—to rotate back so you could touch the wall without any of the compensations occurring, then you'll need to add the prescription exercises that will open up your shoulders. You can find them in chapter 6.

ASSESSMENT TWO—UPPER-BODY ROTATION

If you have limited rotation with your upper body, you're going to start to swing more and more with your arms. At the top of your backswing, you may think you're rotating and turning correctly, but since that rotation is limited, you're really just using your arms. Now, when you swing, you've taken yourself out of true rotation—out of plane. What commonly happens when you're out of plane is that you can't square the club at impact.

If your ball is finding everywhere but the center of the fairway, it may be because you have limited upper-body rotation. Let's find out.

How to do it   Place a stability ball against the wall and sit on it facing away from the wall. Your feet should be flat on the floor and slightly wider than shoulders' width apart. Hold a medicine ball with both hands and assume a golf posture. Try to keep your spine angle the same as it would be if you were out on the golf course. Check out Travis Perkins in Picture 5. He's in the correct starting position.

Remaining in golf posture and with good spine angle, try to touch the ball to the wall by rotating your upper body to your right. Keep your head from

turning and keep your eyes focused on where your ball would be. Avoid pivoting your left foot or allowing your left heel to come off the floor. Also avoid leaning back. Make sure to maintain your spine angle. You want to be able to see your left shoulder directly under your chin. See Picture 6. Hold it for a beat, then return to the starting position. Compensations that your body may make in an attempt to get the ball to touch the wall include your heel coming off the floor and the loss of proper spine angle.

Now rotate to the left. Again, try to touch the ball to the wall. This time, attempt to do it without your right foot coming off the floor, your upper body losing its proper spine angle, or your head being pulled to the left. See Picture 7.

If you weren't able to touch the ball to the wall without losing your spine angle, having your foot pivot, or losing eye contact with your shoulder, guess what? You have limited upper-body rotation. The prescription exercises in chapter 7 may be just what you need to help you loosen up and hit the ball straighter.

7

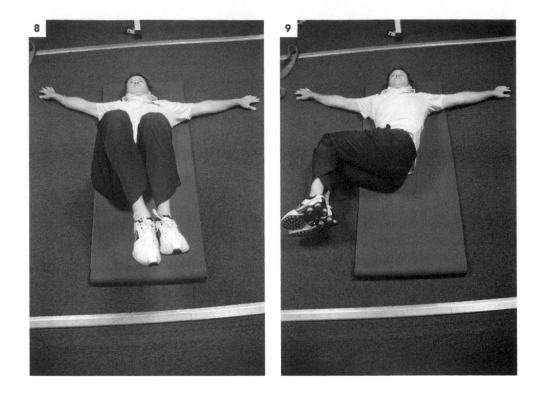

ASSESSMENT THREE—LOWER-BODY ROTATION

Now we're going to check how much separation you have between your upper and lower body. Separation is a good thing. Imagine if there were no separation—whenever your hips turned, your shoulders turned. They wouldn't be able to move independently of each other. This would be an extreme example of having no separation between your upper and lower body. If you've ever severely hurt your back, you know this feeling. It's as if there were an ironing board attached to your back from the base of your hips to the base of your neck.

On the golf course, the lack of adequate separation will limit how far you can confidently and stably rotate in both your backswing and follow-through. This will limit your ability to generate power through your downswing and greatly reduce your accuracy at impact.

Here's an easy way to check if limited lower-body rotation is affecting your ability to outhit your buddies.

How to do it Lie on the floor on your back with your arms out to the sides at shoulder height. Bend your hips and knees to ninety-degree angles so that your thighs are perpendicular to the floor and your lower legs are parallel to the floor. You

should look like you're sitting in a chair—an invisible chair that, for some reason, had been knocked over backward. This is the starting position. Travis Perkins is in the proper starting position in Picture 8.

Without letting your hips slide to the left, drop your legs to the right by rotating your lower body. Ideally, you should be able to drop both legs comfortably to the side so that the outer part of your right leg is flat on the floor, your knees are stacked on top of each other, and your left shoulder is still in contact with the floor. See Picture 9. If your shoulder comes off the floor, that's the compensation that your body is making in an attempt to get the most rotation from your lower body.

Return to the starting position, then slowly try to drop your legs to the left. In a perfect world, you'd be able to have your left leg make complete contact with floor with your knees stacked on top of each other. See Picture 10. Again, look for the ways that your body tries to compensate for tightness.

Could you get your knees to drop to the side? Were you able to keep your shoulders on the floor? If you can't answer yes to both questions, you're ready to let the exercises in chapter 8 help you add distance and accuracy to your game.

ASSESSMENT FOUR—PELVIC TILT AND POSTURE

The key to a consistent and replicable swing is being able to maintain a proper spine angle on your first shot, your twenty-second shot, your fifty-third shot, etc. And the key to a consistent spine angle is strength and stability in the pelvis. If you can't control your pelvis—get it to tilt forward and back when you want it to—you end up with a false spine angle. Your shoulders may be where they need to be at address, but they're only there because you've rounded your back—not because you flexed strongly and confidently at the hips. With a C-shaped posture, you can't stay in plane through impact, and that affects your accuracy. You'll have no idea where your ball is heading. Heck, you might just as well close your eyes and throw a dart at a picture of a golf course.

Let's check your command of your pelvis!

How to do it   Assume an address position—knees slightly bent, proper spine angle, etc. Try to look just like me in Picture 11.

From here, try to tilt your pelvis forward. See Picture 12. Ideally, you should be able to do this without your knees moving or your shoulders. Those are the compensations that your body will make for its inability to control and tilt the pelvis properly. If I wanted you to just stick your butt out, I would have asked you to stick your butt out. Don't worry—a lot of people have difficulty with this assessment. It's a fine movement that isn't addressed in many fitness regimens.

If you weren't able to tilt your pelvis forward and back comfortably—and without the rest of your body moving—you need to check out the exercises in chapter 9. These will help you understand what it takes to control the pelvis and allow you to swing with a truer spine angle and with better accuracy.

ASSESSMENT FIVE—BALANCE

Most people don't think that balance plays much of a role in golf, but if you don't have a strong sense of balance and body awareness, it's going to greatly affect your swing. As you head through your downswing and into impact at full speed, you have to be 100 percent sure where you stand in the universe. If you're not sure whether your weight is moving forward or backward or to the side, an internal survival mechanism kicks in. You begin to decelerate far sooner than you want to because your body is more concerned with not falling over than it is with finding the fairway with your ball. When you decelerate early, you lose clubhead speed and power. You lose distance. Balance equals distance.

Let's check your balance.

How to do it   First, make sure you have plenty of room around you. This one could get interesting. Stand with feet shoulders' width apart and your arms out to your sides at roughly forty-five-degree angles. Slowly raise your right knee in front of you, so that you're balancing on your left foot. Now, close your eyes. Try to hold this one-legged, eyes-closed position for fifteen seconds. See Tim Wilkinson showing off his balance skills in Picture 13.

Open your eyes, shake out your legs, catch your bearings, then try the same thing balancing on your right foot. See Picture 14. Again, shoot for fifteen seconds.

Earlier I said that golfers were some of the greatest compensators in the world. While going through these assessments, you may have noticed the many ways your body compensates for certain weaknesses. What's nice about this balance assessment is that there's no real way for your body to compensate.

You can either stand on one foot—or you can't. Falling down isn't really a form of compensation. If you found yourself staggering around like a college kid at his first keg party, don't worry. That's what chapter 10 is for. Remember, just like strength, endurance, and the ability to speak Chinese, you improve your balance by working on it.

ASSESSMENT SIX—FULL-BODY STRENGTH AND COORDINATION

Parts of your body may be strong and stable individually, and parts may be loose and flexible. As I've pointed out, for the golf swing to happen as it should, all of your parts have to work together. If you can't coordinate the many parts of your body and have them do the things that you want them to do, you can't get the club to do what you want it to do.

I saved this assessment for last because it's the most challenging. It's also the most telling. You will learn a lot about your body from this one.

How to do it   Stand with a stability ball behind your lower back while holding a golf club with both hands. Your arms should be hanging down in front of you, and the club should be parallel to the ground at hip height. Slowly, bend your knees and lower your hips to the floor until your knees are flexed at ninety-degree angles and your thighs are parallel to the floor. Your knees should be aligned over your heels. See Tim Wilkinson in Picture 15.

Keeping your upper body perpendicular to the floor and your arms straight, raise the golf club over your head. See Picture 16. Ideally, you can

raise your arms to the point where your biceps are right next to—or even behind—your ears.

While your body had virtually no way to compensate for lack of balance in Assessment Five—other than to just fall over—you may find no shortage of ways to compensate to try to look like the pictures in Assessment Six. If you were unable to drop into a squat so that your knees were bent at ninety-degree angles, then it tells me you have strength and flexibility issues in your lower body. If you were unable to raise the club directly over your head—or couldn't do it without your elbows bending or your upper body pitching forward—it tells me you have tightness in your upper body. Ultimately what it tells me, though, is that you need the prescription exercises in chapter 11.

ASSESSING THE ASSESSMENTS

That wasn't so bad, was it?

Now that you know what things are preventing your body from doing what it needs to do, it's time to correct them. Fix the body. Fix the swing.

The next six chapters contain the prescription exercises that will help you correct any issues that the assessments revealed. As I mentioned earlier, you'll then combine any prescription exercises with the exercises that I want everyone to be doing. I call them the Joey D. Dozen, and you can find them in chapter 12. Helping you put it all together is chapter 13. That's where I'll tell you how to combine the prescription exercises and the Joey D. Dozen into twenty-minute workouts that will let you fix your body without forcing you to sacrifice all of your time.

Don't be discouraged if you didn't fare as well as you expected on the assessments. They aren't designed to be easy. They are designed to point out areas where your body may have weaknesses. Too many people play it safe by playing only to their strengths—and they never really improve.

Congratulations on having the guts to face your weaknesses.

Now let's do something about them.

6

Shoulder-Rotation Prescription

or . . . Better Accuracy and
Increased Distance. That's All.

When most people think of shoulder muscles, they think of the deltoids. These are the large muscles at the very top of the arm—where the arm connects to the upper body. On heavily muscled athletes, they look like cannonballs. On supermodels, they're the muscles that work in conjunction with the biceps (on the front of the upper arm) and the triceps (on the back of the upper arm) to create a series of sculpted "cuts" at the top of the arm that look so attractive. Whether you're a guy or a gal, well-developed deltoids are hot. The deltoids are sexy muscles.

We're not here to talk about the deltoids.

We're here to talk about some shoulder muscles that you've probably never heard of individually before: the supraspinatus, the infraspinatus, the teres minor, and the subscapularis. Together, they make up the rotator cuff. If you're a sports fan, you've probably heard of the rotator cuff. When you do hear of it, it's rarely in a happy story. Rotator-cuff injuries have ended the careers of many baseball pitchers.

While the deltoids do the heavy work around the shoulder joint—lifting or pressing things overhead, raising the arms, etc.—the rotator cuff does the light work. Extend your arms out directly in front of you with your palms facing the floor. Now, without moving anything else, flip your hands over so that your palms are facing the ceiling. You've just used your infraspinatus and teres minor muscles in your rotator cuff to externally rotate your arm. Now, rotate your palms so that they're facing the floor again. You've just used your subscapularis to internally rotate your arm. Without this ability to fully rotate your arms, you

> I had a tendency to pull a muscle under my scapula—especially when it was cold or when I practiced a lot. I wasn't doing enough of the necessary training to prevent it. The shoulder exercises I do with Joey help me. I feel it the next day, so it must be working. That injury had been happening probably once a month, but 2008 was the best season I've had as a professional. That injury never came back. I feel stronger and I was injury-free and Joey D. had a lot to do with the success.
>
> —*Ryuji Imada, touring professional*

couldn't throw a baseball or a football well. You'd also be at a serious disadvantage out on the golf course.

That's why you're reading this chapter.

So, what happens if you can't rotate your shoulder to the degree that the assessment asked you to do? At the top of your backswing, the ability to externally rotate your arm gives you those few extra degrees of turn. Those few extra degrees translate into more club-head speed and greater power at impact. If your arm stops rotating, you compensate. Again, golfers are the greatest compensators in the world. You know you need to get your arms up to a certain height, but if you can't do it properly—through arm rotation—you get them up there by tilting your body and leaning toward your target. Yes, you've finally got your arms to where they ideally should be, but you've done so at a serious price. You've created a reverse pivot.

All of a sudden, that beautiful golf posture that you started with has been knocked out of balance. The compensation you've made because of your in-ability to rotate your arms enough has thrown off the rest of your game. Be-cause you're off-balance, you're going to spend the rest of your swing worrying about restoring your equilibrium—not concentrating on what you need to be concentrating on. When you swing off-balance, it's difficult to square the club-face at impact. Because you started from a front-leaning, reverse-pivot posi-tion, the odds are you're going to be in front of the ball at impact. Put it all together, and if you're a right-handed player, the ball is usually going to head off to the right.

That's just half of the problem. The inability to externally rotate your arm will also come back to bite you on the other end of your swing. At follow-through, your arm also has to be able to rotate sufficiently. If it can't, your body has to compensate. Because you know that you can't get your arms up to where they need to be for a proper follow-through, you put the brakes on your swing early. Your inability to perform a complete follow-through means that you have less time to stop your club. You can either try to stop a full-speed swing in a reduced amount of time—and run the risk of having your momen-tum pull you off-balance and forward—or you can simply slow down your swing so as to stop your club in that limited time. Generally, you're going to avoid the risk of toppling over clumsily, and instead you're going to decelerate your swing early. This means that you've already reduced your clubhead speed at impact. The result is less power and less distance on your ball.

Loose and strong rotators will let you take advantage of a proper backswing that will keep you in balance and keep your clubface square at impact. They will also let you perform a complete follow-through, so you won't have to decelerate early and sacrifice clubhead speed, and distance, at impact.

For accuracy's and distance's sakes, let's get your rotators healthy.

For the first three exercises, all you'll need are a set of resistance bands. For the fourth, you'll need a stability ball and some light dumbbells.

I was actually shocked about the weaknesses in my shoulders. I had always thought that my left side was a little weaker than my right, but once we started working, I could tell that my shoulders and rotators were really weak. The move that tests external rotation, I couldn't do it with my left shoulder. Everything would sag and my shoulder would go back. It's still a work in progress. Once we got to the point where I was working with Joey for five weeks in a row, though, after about the second week I could feel a noticeable difference—not only in how I felt every day, but in the overall mobility and flexibility in my upper body.
—Travis Perkins, touring professional

I—ONE-ARMED ROW AND ASSISTED ROTATION

This great exercise has some added value. It begins with a rowing motion that will strengthen the large muscles in the back. These muscles are important for helping you create proper posture and proper spine angle at address, and for helping you maintain that posture and spine angle throughout your entire swing. And that's just the bonus part of the exercise!

The guts of the exercise is an assisted version of the shoulder-rotation movement from the assessment chapter. Here, you'll be able to use your opposite arm to help stabilize the arm that's doing the rotation. This will let you completely isolate the rotational motion without having to worry about the arm having to stabilize itself. You'll be able to concentrate on the movement that you need to do and not have to concentrate on keeping your upper arm parallel to the floor or keeping your elbow from moving during the motion. It'll let you really understand what it feels like to use your external rotators.

How to do it

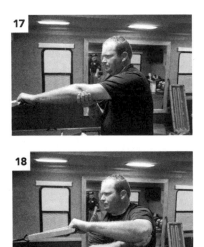

Anchor the band to a solid object at around chest level. Stand facing the anchor point with feet shoulders' width apart and a band handle in your left hand. Raise your left arm straight up in front of you at shoulder height with your palm facing down. Support your arm by holding it under the elbow with your right hand. See Jason Gore demonstrating the starting position in Picture 17. A slight amount of tension should be in the band.

Pull the band back toward you by drawing back your elbow. Your arm should remain parallel to the floor. Draw your elbow back until it is bent at a ninety-degree angle at shoulder height. Because you are still supporting your elbow with your right hand, your left upper arm will be pointing slightly forward from your shoulder. Your forearm should be pointing toward the anchor point with palm facing down. See Picture 18.

Slowly—and I mean slowly—rotate your left forearm up. Use your right hand to help you keep the upper part of your left arm from moving. At the top of the movement, your left forearm should be perpendicular to the floor with your palm facing the anchor point. See Picture 19. Hold for a beat, then return to the starting position.

Even if you only had difficulty with one shoulder during the assessments, I want you to do this exercise with both arms.

II—STANDING EXTERNAL ROTATION

This is another great exercise for strengthening your external rotators. You'll be able to get a slightly greater range of motion around the shoulder than in the first exercise. There, you were limited to 90 degrees of movement. Here, you'll be able to get things into the 110-to-125-degree area. What we're looking for in this chapter is not only to strengthen your rotators, but to get them to move comfortably through a greater range of motion.

That said, don't try to take them through a larger movement at the expense of proper technique. Ultimately, the goal of this program is to get you to reduce the number of compensations that your body is forced to make on the golf course. You're not going to get there if you begin making compensations in the weight room. If you stick with the program, you will develop greater range of motion around the shoulders. Trust me. Do what you can do with proper form and you'll be amazed at the results.

How to do it

Anchor the band to a solid object at between waist and chest height. Stand sideways to the anchor point so that your left ear is facing the anchor point. Hold a band handle in your right hand. Your right forearm should be across the front of your body, facing the anchor point, and parallel to the ground. The upper part of your right arm should be perpendicular to the ground and tight against your side. There should be light tension in the band. See Picture 20.

Keeping your upper arm in place and your forearm parallel to the floor, begin to rotate your right forearm away from the anchor point. Imagine it being a door that's swinging open. See Picture 21.

Rotate it far as you can from the anchor point without the upper part of your right arm moving more than a couple of inches from your body. See Jason Gore in Picture 22. If you want, you can place a folded towel between your body and your upper arm to remind you to hold it close. Hold it for a beat, then return to the starting position.

Again, even if you only had trouble on one side during the assessment, I still want you to do this with both arms.

III—STANDING INTERNAL ROTATION

Fitness is about balance. I'm not just talking about the standing-on-one-foot type of balance. Back in the chapter on biomechanics, I talked about how most muscles and muscle groups have opposing muscles and muscle groups. One muscle will move the body one way, and the opposing muscle will move it the other way. It creates balance and stability for your body's infrastructure and helps you to stay healthy and injury-free.

So, while we've primarily been concerned with your body's ability to externally rotate the arms at the shoulder, we also need to make sure that your body is just as adept at internally rotating the arms at the shoulder as well. An easy and simple exercise will make sure that you're taking care of your internal rotators. It's also a must-do exercise if you plan on doing any competitive arm wrestling.

Because your internal rotators are stronger than your external rotators, you'll be able to use more tension when working them. You can either use a heavier band than you did for the standing external-rotation exercise, or you can just take a step or two farther away from the anchor point.

How to do it   Anchor the band to a solid object at between waist and chest height. Stand sideways to the anchor point so that your right ear is facing the anchor point. Hold a band handle in your right hand. Your right forearm should be angled away from your body, facing the anchor point, and parallel to the ground. The upper part of your right arm should be perpendicular to the ground and tight against your side. Light to moderate tension should be in the band. See Picture 23.

Keeping your upper arm in place and your forearm parallel to the floor, rotate your right forearm away from the anchor point and across your body. See Picture 24. Imagine it's being like a door on a hinge. When it is fully across your body, hold it for a beat, then return slowly to the starting position.

Again, even if you only had trouble on one side during the assessment, I still want you to do this with both arms.

24

25

IV—SHOULDER STABILIZATION ON A STABILITY BALL

Now we're going to hit your rotators in a slightly different way. Before, we worked them through motion. They were forced to rotate a number of degrees while fighting against the resistance provided by the bands. In this exercise, they're going to be forced to hold a static—or nonmoving—position against resistance. It's a great way to develop overall stability around the joint.

Not only are you strengthening your internal rotators by forcing them to hold a position against resistance, you're loosening your external rotators by using the dumbbells as stretching aids. You may not have been able to get your arm to externally rotate ninety degrees on your own, but with the weight of the dumbbells helping out, you may find your shoulders opening up a little more.

A word about the dumbbells. Earlier I told you that for my program I wanted you to use a set of light dumbbells—five pounds each. I was serious. If you decide you want to try this one with a pair of fifteen- or twenty-pound dumbbells, you will hurt yourself. You're reading this chapter because the assessment showed that your rotators are weak. If you attempt this exercise with anything heavier than five-pound dumbbells you will—at best—end up recruiting other muscles in and around the shoulder and not get the results you

want or—at worst—have to schedule surgery. This is a fantastic exercise if you stick with the rules.

How to do it Holding two light dumbbells, lie back on a stability ball so that your shoulders are supported. Raise your hips up slightly so that you feel some tension in your glutes and thighs. Angle your upper arms out directly from your sides at shoulder height. They should be parallel to the floor. Your forearms should be perpendicular to the floor and pointing toward the ceiling. Your palms should be facing in the direction of your feet. See Picture 25.

Slowly—and without moving your upper arms—rotate your forearms back until they are parallel to the rest of your body and the floor. Your elbows should be bent at ninety-degree angles. See Picture 26. Try to keep your upper arms from moving and hold this position for five seconds. You'll feel some tension in your armpit areas, and now you know why I told you to do this with light dumbbells! Slowly rotate your forearms up and return to the starting position to complete the rep. If five seconds is too long, start by just holding the externally rotated position for just a beat until you get used to the movement and the feeling of the exercise.

7 Upper-Body-Rotation Prescription

or . . . Curing Your Arms-Y Swing

Rotation is important. Our very existence is possible because the earth rotates around its axis. Every day it makes one full rotation. If something were to happen to the earth's ability to rotate, we'd all be in trouble. Initially, many of us would be plunged into darkness, while others would be stuck with constant sweltering heat. Eventually, the disruption of the balance and harmony of a normal night-and-day cycle would lead to more serious things: the oceans would dry up, all life would perish, etc.

From a golf perspective, your ability to rotate on the golf course is equally important. While your inability to rotate sufficiently won't necessarily result in the oceans drying up, it will negatively impact your game in a bunch of ways.

If you have a limited ability to rotate your upper body, you will compensate. During takeaway up to the top of your backswing, the body wants to look like the pictures in the magazines. The body wants to look like the players on TV. If it can't rotate, it can't look like the magazine picture or the pro on TV—unless it compensates somewhere. Since you can't rotate back any farther, you raise your arms up. All of a sudden—if you squint—you do sort of look like the guy in the magazine and the guy on TV. What you've done, though, is set yourself up for an arms-y swing. Instead of using your entire body to swing, you're looking at a swing that's going to be primarily driven by the arms. Once that happens, you've taken yourself out of plane. You can't get a true rotation of the body through your downswing and into impact. Now when you swing, it's going to be hard for you to square the club at ball strike. Usually when this happens, the clubface is going to be open. You're going to slice the ball.

> I've always been tight. I'm not hypermobile. Actually, I'm just the opposite. When you have that going on, your ability to rotate becomes limited. For me, the biggest thing I need to do is to try to stay flexible and to try to keep these muscle groups open. We do some strength training, but as far as a week-in week-out type of thing goes, it's about trying to stay open and flexible.
> —Jason Dufner, touring professional

On the other side of your swing, if your body can't rotate properly post-impact, you're going to have to decelerate early to try to maintain your balance. Unfortunately, if it's an arms-y swing, you're going to be out of balance already. Now a different compensation occurs. To try to regain balance from this front-foot-heavy position, you'll try to shift weight to your back foot. Generally, you're going to do this by leaning back and away from your target. This creates a trajectory problem. You're now more likely to pop the ball up instead of hitting it straight. You may take pride in that your ball traveled 250 yards, but if it ends up only 80 yards from where you hit it, you'll have a lot of catching up to do.

So what's preventing you from being able to rotate? A few things. A few very correctable things.

When I talked about the earth, I mentioned that it spun on its axis. Proper golf rotation also happens around an axis—your spine. You've heard such phrases as *golf posture* and *spine angle* a lot. They refer to the proper orientation of the spine that's required to keep your swing on-plane. A lot of the work in this book concentrates on doing the things necessary to make sure that your body can create and maintain a proper spine angle. Here, though, we're concerned with what your body does *around* that proper spine angle.

Generally, two things prevent you from being able to enjoy the required amount of rotation around the spine: weakness in the muscles that actually rotate your body around the spine—the obliques, the semispinalis, the multifidus, and the rotatores—and tightness in the large muscles that make up the upper body—primarily the latissimus dorsi and the pectoralis major. They both need to be addressed. Even if you got your spinal rotators strong, the tightness in your lats and your pecs would act like a brake and prevent proper rotation. And if you got your upper body as loose as it needs to be, you still need the muscles that drive the rotation to be strong. Happily, both of these issues can be addressed at the same time, if you have a workout plan that's been designed creatively and intelligently. And you are holding one in your hands.

Let's get you loose around your axis.

I've been working with Joey for over a year and my body just feels great. I know it definitely helps my performance when my body is in a good place. We do a lot of rotational work and there's definitely a lot more speed in my golf swing, which is what everyone is looking for. You hit the ball farther.
—*Charlie Wi, touring professional*

I—ADDRESS TO BACKSWING WITH MEDICINE BALL

We'll start with a movement that will get your spinal rotators moving in a dynamic way that mimics the movements of the golf swing. This exercise will also help to get the large muscles of your back loose. The key is to keep your butt against the wall the entire time. This will secure one end of your axis line in place and give you a sense of what true rotation at the spine feels like. If you did this away from the wall, it would be too easy to compensate and give yourself a false sense of rotation. By keeping your butt against the wall and your spine angle strong throughout the motion, any movement you do will be pure rotation—with no compensations.

How to do it   Stand at address holding a medicine ball with both hands and with your butt up against a wall. It's important that you try to replicate your true address position as much as possible—arm extension, head position, etc. Don't lean against the wall. The wall is there as a guide to help you keep a true and consistent spine angle; it's not there for you to relax against. See Jason Dufner in Picture 27. Without coming away from the wall, rotate your body to the right—from address through your takeaway and into a modified top-of-backswing position.

27

Ideally, you'll be able to touch the ball to the wall with your hands at about shoulder height. Maintain a solid base and head position. When you look down, you should see your left shoulder directly below your chin. See Picture 28.

If you can't rotate your body to the point where the ball touches the wall, don't worry. Your issues with upper-body rotation are why you're doing the exercises in this chapter. Eventually, you'll be experiencing greater and greater degrees of rotation.

Form is the key, so watch for a few compensations that your body may make. If you come away from the wall, the odds are you'll lose your spine angle. You may be able to get the ball back a little bit farther, but it won't be due to improved upper-body rotation. Similarly, avoid rotating your lower body or pivoting your feet. Again, this may let you get the ball a little bit closer to the wall, but you will have done so by adding a good chunk of lower-body rotation into the mix.

Return to the starting position to complete the rep. To ensure balanced strengthening and stretching, make sure that you also do this exercise rotating to the left.

28

II—IMPACT TO FOLLOW-THROUGH WITH MEDICINE BALL

This is a similar move to the first exercise, but with an important difference. Here you'll be taking your swing through impact and into a modified follow-through. Because your hip pivot will result in your butt coming away from the wall, it's important that you stay aware of your spine angle; the wall won't be serving as your training wheels throughout the entire motion, as it did in the first exercise.

Because adding the pivot is going to give you a greater overall rotation, you'll feel a nice stretch through your middle and upper back. That's a good thing. Remember, in addition to strengthening the muscles responsible for rotating the spine, we also want to make sure that the bigger, more superficial muscles of the upper body—such as your lats—get used to being taken through a greater range of motion. The ball will help. While initially it'll require strength from your spinal rotators to get the ball in motion, once it's moving, you'll be able to use its momentum to assist you in getting a deep stretch for your back.

How to do it Stand with proper spine angle holding a medicine ball with both hands. Your starting position should be just shy of impact. Try to simulate, as much as possible, your true stance at this position. As before, the wall is just there as a guide to help you keep your spine in the proper position; it's not there to lean against. See Jason in Picture 29.

Take your swing through impact and into a modified follow-through. Pivot on your right foot and square your hips toward your imagined target. Try to get the ball to touch the wall at head height. See Picture 30. Don't worry if you can't get it there. As your rotators get stronger and your body gets looser, you'll find yourself getting closer to the wall every time you do this.

Return to the starting position to complete the rep. To make sure that you're working things evenly, also work on your weak-side swing through impact and follow-through.

III—ONE-ARMED ADDRESS TO BACKSWING WITH BANDS

On the surface, this may seem a lot like the first prescription exercise in this chapter—just another simulated takeaway and backswing with something that's clearly not a golf club. On further inspection, though, a lot more is going on.

Because you're not against a wall, you're responsible for creating and maintaining the proper angle of your spine throughout the entire motion. That kicks up the difficulty factor. More important, because you're doing the movement with only one arm and away from a wall, you'll be able to get a deeper rotation. Before, the wall and your left arm's being of a fixed length prevented you from rotating beyond where your hands were at shoulder height. In this exercise, since you'll be doing your takeaway with only your back hand, you'll be able to go deeper. This will work your spinal rotators a little bit more, and you will feel a strong stretch across your pecs and the entire front side of your body.

31

How to do it   Anchor the bands to a solid object at about knee height. Holding a band handle in each hand, assume your address position with good posture, full arm extension, etc. There should be an adequate amount of tension in the bands. See Jason in Picture 31.

Going at the same speed you'd use in your normal swing, start your takeaway by rotating your upper body to the right. Instead of simulating the swing with both arms, do it with just the right. Leave your left arm in place. This will help to remind you to keep a proper spine angle. Rotate your upper body as far as it can go without losing posture and without your lower body starting to turn or pivot. You should feel a stretch through your chest at the top of the motion. See Picture 32. Return to the starting position, then do a takeaway using your left arm.

Up and back with your right arm, then up and back with your left arm, completes one rep.

IV—ONE-ARMED IMPACT TO FOLLOW-THROUGH WITH BANDS

Because you'll be simulating your swing though impact and continuing into your follow-through, you'll be able to get a little bit more rotation thanks to the turning of the hips and the pivoting on the ball of your foot. This will allow you to get an even greater stretch across the front of your body. You should feel this stretch through your abs and chest and up into your armpits and shoulders. This is great for opening up the entire front of your body while strengthening spinal rotators.

How to do it   Anchor the bands to a solid object at about knee height. Holding a band handle in each hand, assume a position with solid golf posture. Make sure there's some tension in the bands. See Jason in Picture 33.

Explosively rotate to the left and simulate impact and follow-through while moving only your left arm. Try to keep your right arm from moving.

Make sure to pivot and turn your hips so that they're be facing where your target would be. You also want to pivot your right foot and come up onto the ball of the foot. At the top of this motion, the angle of "openness" of your arms could be well over 180 degrees. Check out how open Jason's chest is in Picture 34. It looks like he's getting ready to hug the world's fattest man! Don't worry if you can't initially open up your arms that much. Over time, it will happen.

Return to the starting position, then simulate impact and follow-through to the right, moving just your right arm. Up and back to the left, then up and back to the right, completes one rep.

8 Lower-Body-Rotation Prescription

or . . . Discovering Your Hips

Back in the 1950s, a young singer named Elvis Presley was wowing the world with his take on a new style of music called rock and roll. Oddly, though, when he brought his act to national TV, network censors often prohibited the young performer from being shown from the waist down. They felt the movements, thrusts, and gyrations of his hips would be too much for an unsuspecting TV audience. Clearly, they felt the ability to move one's hips through such a broad range of motion with power, timing, and ease was an evil thing—and America had to be protected from witnessing it. Otherwise, heck, everyone would want loose, mobile, and strong hips. That was over fifty years ago. Elvis has, of course, long since up and "left the building," but the ramifications and ripple effect of that decision by network officials can still be seen today on the golf courses of the world: most people don't know how to move their damn hips.

It's just a theory, but if the media hadn't been so nervous about the world seeing a man moving his hips strongly and confidently, this chapter wouldn't have to exist.

Few understand the hips and their important role in both our day-to-day lives and our sporting lives. The hips are to the legs essentially what the shoulders are to the arms. The hips and the shoulders are both ball-and-socket joints. The job of the many muscles that make up the shoulder is to help move and stabilize the arm in numerous planes. They raise your arms to the front and sides; they help you use your arms to do big overhead pushing movements; and they allow you to rotate your arms so that your palms can turn to face up and down. Similarly, the job of the many muscles that make up the hips is to help move and stabilize the legs. They let you raise and lift your legs in all directions; they help you use your legs to jump; and they allow you to rotate your legs so that your feet can pivot.

Even those who aren't necessarily fitness people understand how important it is to train the shoulders in preparation for a sporting activity. Sadly, few folks understand the importance of training the hips. Even those who do incorporate some hip movements in their workouts don't generally incorporate the correct movements. The result is that most people have tight hips, hips that are only strong in certain planes of motion, and hips that cannot work in a coordinated way with the rest of the body.

Those shortcomings may not be evident when you're just hanging around at home or working at the office. But on the golf course, those issues get magnified greatly, and they will make playing the game a whole lot less fun and rewarding.

If you can't get your lower body involved properly in your takeaway into your backswing, you end up becoming a upper-body-dominant player. When your lower body won't rotate, you naturally compensate by forcing your upper body to do all of the work. The arms-y swing that results is going to lack a lot of power. It makes sense when you realize you're only using half of your body to perform a full-body movement. If you can't get your lower body to help you develop power, you might as well carry a folding chair with you the next time you head out to the golf course. Set it up right where you would normally stand at address, have a seat, get all comfortable, then do a big old arms-only swing. That's only a slight exaggeration of what it's like to be incapable of involving your lower body correctly in the early part of your swing.

If you can't get your lower body to play along through impact, your timing is also going to be off. Your upper body and your lower body are going to be on two different pages, and it will affect your balance. Once your balance and timing are thrown off, it becomes hard to sync everything up at impact. Usually your clubface won't be squared. You won't know if your clubface will be open or closed when you strike the ball. It won't be a mystery for long, though. The everywhere-but-straight-ahead path of your ball will tell you if you were open or closed at impact.

The key to avoiding these problems is to get the muscles that make up the hips to be strong and loose. The more we can take things in that direction, the less of an upper-body player you'll be. You'll be able to strike the ball with more power. You'll also be confident that the added distance that you'll be getting from that power boost is distance in the correct direction.

Make "the King" proud. Let's work on your hips.

My hips are tight and we'd had a tough time getting them to where they were a little looser and could move the way my instructor at the time wanted my hips to move. I always just did your basic stretches. I never really had a trainer before Joey D., but he just knew the ways to open the hips up and get them looser for me so I could get them to move the way that I wanted them to move. It wasn't easy, but he just has the knowledge.

—*John Rollins, touring professional*

I—HIP TURN WITH MEDICINE BALL

This is a lot like the assessment test you did for checking lower-body rotation, but with one major difference that's going to impact things in a couple of different ways. You're going to do this exercise while holding a medicine ball between your knees. This means your hips will go through a slightly reduced range of motion. During the assessment, for example, you may have found that you were able to turn and drop your right leg to the side without your left shoulder coming up off the floor. When you tried to get your left leg to stack on top of your right leg, perhaps your shoulder got pulled off the floor. Here, because the ball is preventing your left leg from being able to stack directly on top of the right leg, you may find your body able to perform the move properly. Over time, it will lead to the loosening and lengthening of the muscles that were preventing you from passing the assessment.

The medicine ball will also strengthen your hips, spinal rotators, and core. You're not simply just raising your legs from the side-turned position back to the knees-straight-up starting position—as you did in the assessment. Now,

you're dealing with eight pounds of resistance while you're doing it. You also have to keep a firm squeeze on the medicine ball to hold it in place. Just about every known law of physics will back me up when I say that you definitely don't want to loosen your grip on the ball when you're in the knees-straight-up position.

How to do it Lie back on the floor or on a mat with your legs bent and a medicine ball squeezed between your knees. Place your arms out to your sides, palms down, to help stabilize you. Raise your legs by flexing at the hips. Your thighs should be perpendicular to the floor and your lower legs should be parallel to the floor. Both your hips and knees should be flexed at ninety degrees. See Jason Gore in Picture 35.

Slowly drop your hips to the right side until the outer part of your right leg touches the floor. Try to keep your left shoulder from coming up off the floor. See Picture 36. Hold for a beat, then slowly return to the starting position.

Don't drop the ball—it will negatively impact more than just your golf game!

Hold the knees-straight-up position for a beat, then slowly drop your knees to the left side. Try to get the outer part of your left leg to touch the floor without your right shoulder lifting off the floor. See Picture 37. Hold for a beat, then return to the starting position to complete the rep.

II—2:00 TO 10:00 ROLLOVER WITH STABILITY BALL

This is a great movement that will really let you feel what it's like to rotate your lower body. You'll feel this deep into your glutes and into your lower back. If you get into this one, you're going to want to start driving around with a stability ball wedged into your car. After a few hours behind the wheel, no stretch feels better for the body than this one.

On the strength and coordination side, having to control the ball will force you to recruit your hip adductors on the inside part of your upper thigh, as well as your hamstrings and even your calves. Any movement that gets all of these body parts to work together for a common good is a step in the right direction.

That said, you want to pay strict attention to form. Your body can compensate in a lot of ways when you perform this movement.

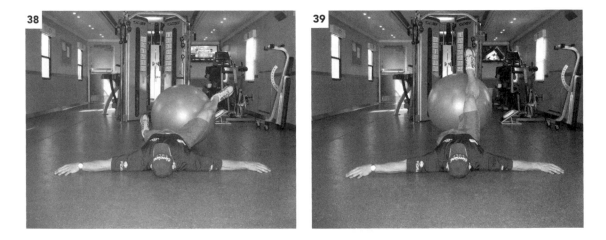

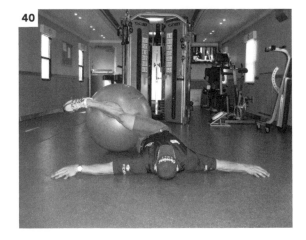

How to do it Lie on the floor with a stability ball between your legs and your arms extended straight out to the sides. Drape your right leg over the ball. If from your vantage-point the ball were a clock and the top of the ball represented 12:00, drape your leg over the ball at what would be 2:00. See me showing off my clock-reading skills in Picture 38. Note that my left leg is extended straight down in a perfectly straight line that extends from my left heel to the top of my head.

Secure the ball using your hamstrings, calf, and the muscles on the inside of your right thigh, then slowly rotate the ball over your left leg. Try to do this without your right shoulder coming up off the floor. Going back to the if-the-ball-were-a-clock concept, you want to roll the ball over your left leg by having it appear that your right leg is turning back time and going from 2:00 to 12:00 and eventually to 10:00. I'm halfway through motion—or at 12:00—in Picture 39.

Continue rotating until your right leg is now at 10:00. See Picture 40. If you're doing it correctly and your left leg is still straight and your right shoulder is still in contact with the floor, you should be feeling a great stretch. If you were unable to rotate all the way to 10:00 without your shoulder coming off the floor, don't worry. Rotate as far as you can without your shoulder moving. Eventually, you will get it to the 10:00 position. Hold this final position for a three-count, then slowly reverse the movement until you are back to the 2:00 starting position.

Make sure that after you do this using your right leg on the ball, you also do it with your left leg on the ball.

III—CONTINUOUS HIP TURNS OVER STABILITY BALL

This is a similar motion to the hip turn with the medicine ball, but with an important difference. Instead of breaking the movement down into segmented ninety-degree hip turns, here you don't have to start and stop from a neutral knees-up position between rotations. This continuous side-to-side motion will let your body understand and feel what it has to do to integrate your lower body with your upper body during your golf swing.

How to do it

Lie on the floor with both legs draped over a stability ball and your arms extended straight out to the sides. The ball should be right up against your thighs, and if the ball were a clock, your legs should be draped over it at what would be 10:00 and 2:00. See Picture 41.

Without letting your left shoulder come up off the floor, rotate your hips and the ball as far as you can to the right. Ideally, you'll be able to get the outside of your right leg to touch the floor. If you can't, just rotate as far as you can without your left shoulder lifting. See Picture 42.

As soon as you've rotated as far as you can to the right, reverse the rotation and rotate your hips and the ball to the left. Again, shoot for getting the outside of your left leg to touch the floor without your shoulder lifting. If that's just not going to happen, just rotate as far as you can while keeping your shoulders flat on the ground. See Picture 43.

You may find that you can rotate fully to one side and not the other. That's natural. You've had your entire life to create imbalances within your body. This exercise is just one of the ways to get you back in balance.

9

Pelvic-Tilt and Posture Prescription

or . . . Align Your Spine

The goal of most fitness programs is to get your body to do big things with heavy weights. You bench-press hundreds of pounds to develop a strong and powerful chest, and you do squats with a heavily loaded barbell across your upper back to strengthen your legs. Compared to those feats of strength, what I'm trying to get you to do in this chapter may seem a bit mundane. I just want you to be able to tilt your pelvis forward and back. In the grand scheme of human movement, that's not asking a whole lot. I don't want you to push my car around the block or swim a mile with a cinder block tied to each leg. All I want you to do is to comfortably and confidently move your pelvis an inch or two.

While being able to move your pelvis the length of a golf tee may not seem like such a lofty accomplishment, out on the golf course the price you pay for not being able to do it is steep.

If you cannot tilt your pelvis forward, you can't have a true and proper spine angle. End of statement. The ability to tilt your pelvis is the first in a chain of events that must occur if you are to stand at address with good golf posture and then swing a club with true rotation. A strong pelvis and core are the foundations that your golf posture is built upon.

When you tilt your pelvis forward, you allow your body to flex correctly at the hips. This slight kicking back of your hips will let you keep your back straight and assume a comfortable and correct posture at address. If you can't get your pelvis to cooperate, your body will start to compensate. Without correct—or possibly any—flexion at the hips, you have to compensate to get your upper body to be where it needs to be when you step up to the ball. You do this by curving the back and spine.

What happens when you try to swing with a curved back? Heck, your guess is as good as anyone's.

We're going to play with some pasta to let you see all the perils of playing with a curved—or C-shaped—spine. Imagine holding a dry piece of penne—that's the tubular pasta with the lines down the side—between your thumb and your forefinger. Rub your fingers back and forth to make the pasta rotate. Do you see how true and clean that rotation is? That's how your swing looks when you start with—and maintain—a proper spine angle. Now, imagine holding a dry piece of elbow macaroni in your fingers and rotating it between your thumb and forefinger. That's what your swing looks like when you have a rounded, C-shaped spine. It's an uneven, irregular, and warped rotation. Okay, we can stop playing with our food now.

When you attempt to swing with a rounded back, you can't stay in-plane. Your swing becomes unpredictable, and you will suffer all sorts of accuracy issues. If we can straighten out your spine, we can straighten out your shot. But the only way we're going to be able to do that is by getting you to tilt your pelvis and create the necessary stability in the pelvis, hips, and core.

To get you to tilt your pelvis we're going to be focusing on some muscles that you've been using all of your life—your latissimus dorsi in the back of the body, and your obliques and rectus abdominus in the front of your body. Just because you've used them before doesn't mean that you'll be able to figure out how to get them to tilt your pelvis, though. You're doing the exercises in this chapter because you had trouble getting your pelvis to tilt during the initial assessment. Your job is to take these muscles that you're already familiar with and, essentially, teach some old dogs a new trick.

It's not an unattainable goal. This motion may seem impossible at first, but that's only because it's a brand-new movement for a lot of you. Think about it: you've been able to live your life, do well in business, and operate as a responsible and functioning member of society—all without anyone ever asking you to move your pelvis. Of course it's going to seem new and strange to try to do something that's, well, new and strange. I've found, though, that a lot of players have a "lightbulb moment" when it comes to pelvis tilting. One minute it just isn't happening, then the next minute you can almost see a light go on inside them and they're able to do the movement.

But you're never going to learn to tilt your pelvis simply by reading about it. Let's get to work strengthening your pelvis, fixing your posture, and straightening out your shot.

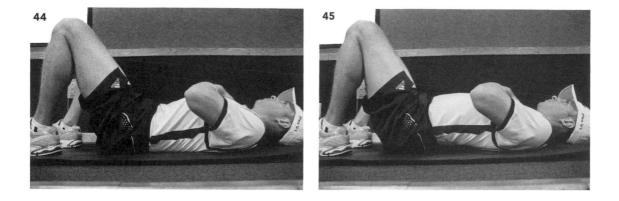

I—PELVIC TILT ON MAT

This is a great way to really understand what it means to tilt your pelvis. Instead of just guessing and wondering if you can move your body correctly, you'll have easy-to-see and easy-to-feel proof. If you're able to create a space between your lower back and the floor, you now know you have the ability to move your pelvis. That's a super start. Eventually, of course, you'll need to master the movement so it transfers to the golf course. You have to walk, though, before you can run.

How to do it   Lie on the floor on a mat with your knees bent and your arms crossed over your chest. Press your lower back into the floor. Try to make contact with the floor with the entire length of your back. If you're having trouble, try exhaling as you press your lower back down. If you got your lower back all the way to the floor, it means you successfully tilted your pelvis back. Congratulations! In Picture 44, here's what it looks like when Tim Wilkinson presses his lower back into the mat.

Now, you're going to try to tilt your pelvis forward. Instead of pressing your lower back into the floor, I want you to create a space between the floor and the small of your back. See Picture 45. If you got your lower back off the floor, again congratulations! The only way you could do this was by tilting your pelvis forward. Every time you press down and come up is one rep. The more you do this, the easier it will get. Ideally, you get to the point where you can slide your hand under your lower back when it's in the "up" position.

II—HIP DROP ON STABILITY BALL

This big motion will, in addition to getting you to continue to move your pelvis, also work some other things in and around the hips.

At the top of the motion, you may feel your glutes tightening. Strong glutes will help you maintain a solid base at setup and address and give you more control over your lower body throughout your entire swing. You might also feel a stretch in your hip flexors. These are the muscles at the very top of each leg. Their job is to raise your leg up in front of you. Because of the way we live our lives—we sit down most of the time and don't stretch enough—most of us have hip flexors that are too tight. Off the golf course, tight hip flexors can lead to poor posture and lower-back pain. On the golf course, tight hip flexors will affect your ability to get your hips and lower body involved in your swing. Once you take your lower body out of the equation, you become an upper-body-dominant player, and both your power and accuracy will suffer.

How to do it   Lie back on a stability ball with your upper back and shoulders comfortably supported. Your feet should be about shoulders' width apart with your knees aligned directly over your heels. Dip your hips down so that your tailbone is about three or four inches from the ball. At the bottom of the movement, try to tilt your pelvis forward, as if you were trying to kick your hips back and touch the ball with your tailbone. Keep your knees above your heels and don't let the ball roll. See Picture 46.

From here, you're going to straighten your body by raising your hips until your entire body—from your knees to your head—is essentially parallel to the floor. See Picture 47. Be aware of not just raising your hips, but also of trying to get your pelvis to tilt backward. Because you are on your back, this would mean that you're trying to get the lower part of your pelvis to be slightly higher than the top of your pelvis. Try to be strong and stable in the position—as if you were a piece of solid furniture. Hold this "up" position for a beat, then drop your hips back down into the starting position to complete the rep.

III—PELVIC DIP ON STABILITY BALL

This may look a lot like the hip drop, but it's a lot finer movement and may be a little more challenging. Here, you're not dropping and raising your entire hip area, you're just tilting your pelvis forward and back. This one may take some getting used to, and you may feel that you're just lying on a stability ball doing "something" with your hips until you become more comfortable with the movement. Stick with it, though. If you can confidently move your pelvis in this position, you will be more than ready to transfer that ability out onto the golf course. The only thing your friends will know is that you're now standing up straighter, swinging with more confidence, and finding the fairway more. They won't know that you got that way by doing pelvic thrusts on a stability ball.

How to do it   Lie back on a stability ball with your upper back and shoulders comfortably supported. Your feet should be about shoulders' width apart with your knees aligned directly over your heels. Tilt your pelvis forward slightly. This will kick your hips back and cause you to stick your butt out—and in this case, down—a bit. You might feel your back arch slightly. I'm not looking for a giant movement here. In fact, if you move more than a couple of inches, it means that you're probably just dropping your hips—and not tilting your pelvis. Here I am tilting my pelvis in Picture 48.

You're now going to reverse the position by tilting your pelvis back. This will bring your hips back up, and you may feel your back rounding or lengthening. See Picture 49. In this position, everything from your knees to your head is parallel to the ground. Hold this "up" position for a beat, then drop your hips back down into the starting position to complete the rep.

Balance Prescription

or . . . Finding New Power

Balance is one of the least understood and least appreciated elements of the golf game. People assume that because they can stand on two feet, they have the balance that it takes to swing a club. In a way, they're correct. They can stand on two feet and, yes, they can swing a club. But can they swing a club the same way as a player who has trained his sense of balance and who knows what his body is doing at every stage of the golf swing? Probably not. Can they possibly be aware of all of the postural compensations that they make because of their lack of balance and body awareness? Again, probably not. Can they ever dream of being able to get rid of those compensations without understanding the importance of balance and without working to develop an improved sense of balance? Definitely not.

It's amazing. Over 1 trillion exercise and fitness books are out there, and few even mention balance.

Could Michael Jordan have done what he did without an incredible sense of balance? Could he have left the ground knowing exactly how much pressure to use to push off with each of his feet, thread—in midair—through opposing defenders on his way to the net, then land—featherlight—on his feet after another highlight-reel dunk without an absurdly keen sense of where his body was in relation to his environment?

Could Greg Maddux—who won four consecutive Cy Young Awards and who notched at least fifteen wins in seventeen straight seasons—possibly have had as much control over his pitch speed, pitch placement, and pitch movement if he hadn't understood precisely how important a role balance played in the ability to hit a small target with a ball from sixty feet six inches away?

Whether you're the greatest basketball player of all time or the greatest finesse pitcher of all time, to play at the top of your game, you need to know exactly how your body—in motion—fits into the world around you.

It's no different on the golf course. The game's greats have an uncanny sense of balance. At the Tour Academy, we have some pretty nice toys. To measure a player's balance and body awareness we have a special plate that he stands on while swinging. It measures the front-to-back and left-to-right shifting of his center of gravity, and it lets us see exactly where a player's weight is distributed during the various parts of the swing. For the top players, it's a smooth line that travels to their back foot, then forward to their front foot. It's to the point where I can tell just by looking at the readout of their center of gravity how sound their swing is.

While the on-screen display of a touring pro's weight distribution is a clean and predictable path from address to follow-through, the center of gravity readings for just about everyone else can be off the charts. Instead of being a concise line that shows awareness and body control, it can be a meandering, herky-jerky set of squiggles that looks more like the results of a polygraph test that had been administered to a pathological liar.

What happens if you don't have good balance on the golf course? It doesn't matter if you're off-balance and leaning back, off-balance and leaning forward, or off-balance and leaning to either side, you're going to create deceleration. When you're out of balance and have to control a clubhead that's traveling 100-plus mph, you no longer have the luxury of being able to concentrate on the things you'd like to be concentrating on—maintaining good spine angle, making sure your clubface is square at impact, eating the turkey sandwich you have in your golf bag. When you're out of balance, all your body really wants to do is reestablish your balance—and the easiest way to do that is to slow down that runaway train of a golf club. You've created chaos, and now you're forced to do whatever it takes to try to control it. So you decelerate. You step on the brakes far earlier than you would have wanted to. Your clubhead speed at impact is greatly reduced, and the result is a whole lot less distance on your ball. On the bright side, though, you didn't fall over!

Most people assume that they can't do anything to improve their balance. They figure it's like the weather—it is what it is and there's not a lot you can do about it. They're wrong. Just like strength, endurance, agility, coordination, and how well you cook, you get better at balance by working on your balance.

Balance training is unlike the rest of the training that makes up my program. The rest of the program deals with your body's "hardware." You create strength and greater range of motion around the shoulders to be able to rotate your arms back to where they need to be in your backswing, and you build strength around your hips and pelvis to achieve and maintain proper golf posture. It's about physically changing your body. Working on balance, though, deals more with your body's "software." Physical and mechanical benefits will result from the balance training you'll be doing; you'll develop more strength and stability around the ankles, knees, and hips, for example. The majority of the benefits, though, will be more neurological than physical.

To understand that, we need to learn just what the heck is responsible for our sense of balance in the first place.

Your sense of balance is a result of three different systems in your body. Your inner ear has a series of looping canals that sort of look like the confusing configuration of highway connections that you're forced to deal with whenever you rent a car in a strange city. The movement of fluid inside those canals helps you deal with—and respond to—rotational movement. Also inside your ear are your otolithic organs, which help you interpret linear movement. Together, they make up the vestibular system.

Your muscles also play a role in balance. In addition to helping you do such things as run, jump, and putt, your muscles also have a sense of where they are in relation to your other body parts. If I told you to close your eyes and punch yourself in the head, you could. Your fist knows where your head is. This proprioceptive ability is good for more than just giving you the confidence to—if you needed to—punch yourself in the head with your eyes closed, though. This same ability to figure out where all of your body parts are and how they need to move to deal with the rigors of a three-dimensional world is the second system that the body uses to keep upright.

The third system that you use for maintaining balance is your vision. If you're reading this and have to do the balance prescription exercises, I'm guessing you found that out the hard way. It was probably easy enough to stand on one foot with your eyes open, but once you closed your eyes and couldn't lock onto a fixed point in the room, all hell broke loose. Combined, all three of these systems work to help you figure out where you—and all of your body parts—are in the world.

Now that you know some of the science behind our amazing ability to not constantly fall down, it's time to improve your balance. On the golf course, better balance will let you be a lot more stable and secure throughout your entire swing and keep you from having to decelerate early due to your loss of equilibrium. That'll lead to more distance on every shot.

I—ONE-LEGGED GOLF POSTURE

One reason that people lose their command of balance during their swing is that the whole movement begins from a forward-leaning position. You may have great balance when you're standing up straight on two feet, but once you assume golf posture, your center of gravity is pitched forward. This is a great drill for helping you get used to maintaining balance in golf posture. Heck, if you can do it on one foot, doing it on two feet when you're out on the course will be a snap.

How to do it Stand comfortably with feet about shoulders' width apart and your hands by your side. Okay, that was the easy part—it's about to get tough. Flex your left knee to a ninety-degree angle until the lower part of your left leg is in back of you and parallel to the ground. Only the lower part of your left leg should have moved. Your thighs should still be parallel to each other. Check out Picture 50 to see how it's done.

From here, I want you to slowly and confidently flex forward at the hips and assume golf posture with good spine angle and arm extension. See Picture 51. Hold for five seconds, then slowly return to the standing one-legged position. Hold that position for a beat to show that you are able to maintain your balance through movement, then bring your left foot back to the ground. That's one rep.

Of course, it's not enough just to develop killer balance on your right leg. Make sure to do an equal amount of work balancing on your left leg.

Once this drill becomes too easy—which I'm confident it eventually will—do it while holding a light dumbbell. Pictures 52 and 53 show me demonstrating this advanced variation.

11—ONE-LEGGED ADDRESS TO TAKEAWAY

Now it's getting fun. It was one thing to come into golf posture on one leg and then hold a static position; it's another thing to come into a forward-leaning position on one leg and then further mess with your equilibrium by having you rotate your body. What this does is force you to deal with a constantly shifting center of gravity as you take your position from address to takeaway. This one may take a few attempts before you start nailing it with consistency and confidence. What's nice, though, is that once you do get the hang of it, you'll have concrete proof that your sense of balance is getting better. That's progress—and progress is good.

How to do it Assume a one-legged address position. Do everything you'd do on the golf course—maintain proper spine angle, arm extension, head position—just do it on one foot! See Tom Pernice Jr. in Picture 54.

Now, while still on one foot and with proper posture, start your swing. Take your hands back to about shoulder height. This isn't easy. When you get good at it, you'll look just like Tom in Picture 55. Look at the rotation of the upper body and the position of his head. His eye is still on his ball. Slowly return to address. Hold a one-legged address for a beat, then lower your raised foot to the ground to complete the rep.

Remember, if you started the exercise by balancing on your left foot, you're going to finish it by balancing on your right foot.

III—ONE-LEGGED IMPACT TO FOLLOW-THROUGH

This one is going to be even more challenging. In the one-legged address to takeaway, you were doing your best to simulate your regular swing, which means that you should have kept your eye on your ball the whole time. Remember, balancing is a heck of a lot easier when you can fix your visual focus on a nonmoving point. Without that visual cue to help fix you in your place in the world, staying upright is a lot harder. That's why I had you close your eyes during the assessment. Here, since you are simulating impact through follow-through, your focal point has to change. You have to go from looking at your ball to watching it travel—dead center—down the fairway.

Just a heads-up—this one may be trickier than you expect. Again, though, when you do get a feel for this movement, you'll have more evidence that your balance is improving. And when you get really good at it, it's a nifty trick that'll let you have some fun with your golf pals. Demonstrate how easily you can do the move, then challenge them to do it. Put some money on it. Unless they've been doing some golf-specific balance training—which they haven't—there's no way they're going to nail this. Heck, you'll be able to make back the cost of this book from this one exercise alone!

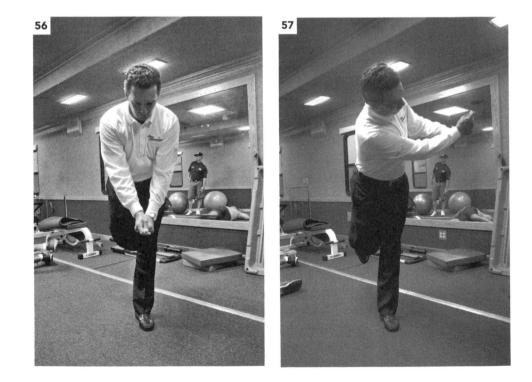

How to do it   Assume a one-legged golf posture. Again, be aware of all the things that you'd be mindful of on the golf course—spine angle, arm extension, your eye on your ball, etc. See Picture 56.

Now imagine that you'd just hit your ball. While still on one foot, rotate your upper body as you would in your follow-through and direct your gaze a virtual 325 or 350 yards away—or where you'd normally expect to see your drive wind up. Again, this one isn't easy. Taking your eye off a fixed point when you're trying to balance can be a one-way ticket to the floor. Check out Tom in Picture 57, though. He did this in one take! You think it's just a coincidence that he has such good balance and can play the game as well as he can?

Return from the follow-through position to the starting position. Maintain a solid one-legged golf posture for a beat, then return your raised foot to the ground to complete the rep.

Remember, whatever you do on one leg, you have to do on the other leg.

IV—ONE-LEGGED CHEST OPENER

There's a lot of bang for the buck with this one. Since just about everyone can use help with his balance, and since just about everyone can also benefit from a chest-opening stretch, there's not much downside to this drill.

How to do it   Stand with feet shoulders' width apart and your hands by your side. Slowly bend your right knee to a ninety-degree angle so that the lower part of your right leg is parallel to the floor. Your thighs should still be parallel to each other. See Picture 58.

Extend your arms straight up overhead and tilt your head back slightly so your gaze moves toward the ceiling. See Picture 59.

Finally, lean back as if you were aiming your chest at the ceiling. See Picture 60. You should feel a good stretch through your chest and into your shoulders. Try to hold this position for five seconds. Return to the initial one-legged position. Hold for a beat, then bring your raised foot down to complete the rep.

Just like all the rest of these balance prescription exercises, you're going to do this on each leg.

11 Full-Body Strength and Coordination Prescription

or . . . Mr. Upper-Body, Please Meet Mr. Lower-Body

The majority of this book—and my program—is about identifying and isolating individual problems and then correcting them. We want your pelvis to tilt, your shoulders to externally rotate more, your hips to turn, etc. This, fittingly, is the last prescription chapter, and it deals with more of a "big picture" look at your body. It's great to be strong and it's great to be flexible, but out on the golf course, you must combine that strength and flexibility. The assessment for full-body strength and coordination checked to see how well your upper body and lower body played with each other. Sometimes you can be strong with your lower body and loose with your upper body, but when you try to integrate your feet, legs, hips, core, chest, shoulders, arms, and every other little thing in your golf swing, something mysterious happens. You're unable to muster all the lower-body strength that you had or take advantage of all the upper-body range of motion you had.

If you had trouble with the overhead-raise assessment, it means that your shoulders are protracted forward and that you're unable to create or maintain a proper posture throughout your swing. You'll have a C-shaped instead of a straight spine, and that will prevent you from ever setting up with a proper spine angle. That takes you out of plane almost as soon as you start your takeaway. And it can only get worse from there. If you're out of plane, you're not swinging the club with true rotation. Rotational problems, as I've pointed out, show up

> For the past three years, I've been trying to get into certain positions in my golf swing, and it's been difficult. I can get there, but it doesn't repeat itself. I saw my teacher after not seeing him for almost seven months, and he was amazed at the positions I was getting into. And we could go ahead and work with these positions, where before we would talk about them, but I could never get to them. Now he was putting me into these positions and there was absolutely no strain on my body whatsoever.
>
> —*Travis Perkins, touring professional*

on the course as accuracy problems. If you're not sure exactly how your body is going to rotate, you can't know exactly how you're going to strike the ball.

If you had trouble with the lower-body assessment and weren't able to drop your hips down so your knees were bent at ninety-degree angles and your thighs were parallel to the ground, you have strength and stability issues in the legs and hips. Your glutes and your quadriceps—the large groups of muscles in the fronts of your thighs—are weak. This will haunt you at setup and address. You won't be able to get in the position you need to be in, and you'll be too stiff-legged and straight up.

When this part of your initial posture is wrong, the wheels fall off pretty quickly. Similar to the problems that result from a protracted, C-shaped posture, you won't be able to find the correct plane line. This will lead to accuracy problems. You'll also have trouble getting into the proper position at the top of your backswing. You'll have a false sense of range of motion—you're not getting the club to where you think you are—and end up with a three-quarters swing. Your goal on the golf course isn't to take a half or three-quarters swing. Your goal is to take a full swing. That can happen only if all of the parts of your body are strong through a great range of motion individually and can also maintain that strength through that range of motion while working as a unit.

By integrating your upper-body movements with your lower-body movements, you'll be more prepared to handle what your entire body needs to do on the golf course. You'll be able to correct postural issues and will hit the ball straighter and with more confidence and power. More important, this full-body coordination will allow you to do things on the golf course that you previously just weren't able to do.

I—AIR BENCH

The air bench is a great way to strengthen your entire lower body while forcing you to be aware of your core and of your posture. It's the only exercise in my program that doesn't involve any movement. That doesn't mean that it's easy or that it's not effective. It does mean, though, that unlike all the other exercises, which are divided into repetitions, here you'll just do one rep. Initially, try to hold the position for twenty seconds. From then on, every time you do this exercise, try to add ten seconds. Eventually, you'll get so strong doing it you may actually fall asleep in this position.

How to do it Place a stability ball between you and the wall and slowly drop your hips down until your thighs are parallel to the floor. Your knees should be bent at ninety-degree angles and should be aligned over your heels. The ball should be behind your middle and lower back and your spine should be straight. See Picture 61.

Just stay there. The first time you do it, shoot for twenty seconds, but add ten more seconds every time you do it. Don't sacrifice the technique for the sake of longer times, though. Your body will make certain compensations as it gets tired. Make sure that your thighs stay parallel to the floor and that your knees and hips are at the same height. Also make sure that your back stays straight. As time goes on, your body is going to want to slouch forward. Don't let that happen.

11—SEATED OVERHEAD EXTENSION

This may just look as if Travis Perkins is raising a club over his head because, well, that's all he is doing. Don't be fooled, though. This is a great way to open up the chest and shoulders, and if you had trouble with that aspect of the assessment, this simple movement will, eventually, let you get your arms where you need them to be out on the golf course.

You'll notice that while you're doing this, your core has to stay strong—otherwise you're going to lose your posture. As your core gets stronger, not only will it be easier to maintain your posture while doing movements such as this overhead extension, it'll be easier to maintain your posture and spine angle when you're out on the golf course.

How to do it   Sit on a stability ball with your feet slightly wider than shoulders' width apart. Hold a golf club in front of you with your arms straight. Your hands should be about the same distance apart as your feet. See Picture 62.

Keeping your arms straight and your elbows from bending, extend the club over your head. The key is to get the club directly over your head. Ideally, your biceps are side by side with your ears—or even in back of them. See Picture 63. Try to maintain a straight back and avoid leaning or pitching your upper body forward. Remember, the goal is to bring your biceps to your ears—not your ears to your biceps. Hold the club in the "up" position for a beat, then return to the starting position to complete the rep.

III—FORWARD LUNGE WITH OVERHEAD EXTENSION AND ROTATION

This might just be the exercise with the longest name in my whole program, but it's also one of the best. This is just a superb way to strengthen and stretch the lower body while you also open up the chest and shoulders and work on your ability to rotate. Oh, and you'll also be working on your core and balance as well. Most parts of your body have a role to play in this one. It's earned its really long name.

How to do it

Start with feet shoulders' width apart while holding a golf club in front of you with straight arms. The club should be parallel to the ground at hip height, and your hands should be slightly wider than shoulders' width apart. See Picture 64.

Step forward deeply with your right leg into a lunge position. At the same time, keeping your arms straight and your elbows from bending, raise the club overhead. You *need* to look for a few things in this position and *want* to look for a few others.

Necessities first. It's important that in the lunge position your lead knee is aligned over your lead heel. If the knee slides too far over the foot, it can put a lot of pressure on the knee. We don't want that. In fact, it's the exact opposite of that we want. We want your knees to be happy and healthy.

The things that you *want* to look for in this position are to make sure that the club is directly overhead and that your shoulders are aligned over your hips. This means that you're doing as much as you can to open up the chest and shoulders, while also working on your posture and lower-back strength. Check out Ryuji Imada in Picture 65 to see how you should look in the lunge position.

From here, keeping your arms extended directly over your head and your shoulders positioned directly over your hips, rotate your upper body in the direction of your lead leg—in this case, that means to the right. Try to keep your hips squared forward. See Picture 66.

Hold this position for a beat, then return to the lunge position—with the club still raised overhead. Finally, push off the right leg and lower the club as you return to the original starting position. One lunge and twist on the right side and one lunge and twist on the left side equals one rep.

IV—REVERSE LUNGE WITH OVERHEAD EXTENSION

Unless you work for the Department of Motor Vehicles, you probably don't do a whole lot of things completely backward. You may want to practice stepping back a few times before you try stepping back into a full lunge. When you do get comfortable with the motion, it'll become a great way to develop leg and core strength and help you open up your chest and shoulders. It'll also be a real boost for your balance. If you didn't read the chapter on balance, you really should. Balance is one of the most important, but least understood, attributes to have out on the golf course.

How to do it   Start with feet shoulders' width apart while holding a golf club in front of you with straight arms. The club should be parallel to the ground at hip height, and your hands should be slightly wider than shoulders' width apart. See Picture 67.

Carefully step backward with your left leg into a lunge position. You'll need to step back deep enough so that when you hit the lunge position, your front knee—in this case, your right knee—is aligned over your front heel. At the same time, keeping your arms straight and your elbows from bending, raise the club overhead.

Make sure the front knee stays over your front heel and that it doesn't slide over your toes or beyond. Try to get the club directly overhead without bending your arms. If you have any doubt as to what you should look like in this position, use Ryuji Imada in Picture 68 as your role model.

Hold this lunge position for a beat, then push off the back foot and return to the starting position as you lower the club back to hip height.

12

The Joey D. Dozen

or . . . the Twelve Secrets
of the Pros

Now that you've gone through the assessments and have figured out what prescription exercises you need to do to fix your body so you can fix your swing, it's time to meet the other half of the program. I call it the Joey D. Dozen—twelve exercises that everyone should be doing. And next to properly tipping your caddie and replacing your divots, these are probably the twelve most important things a golfer can do.

If you've gone through fitness programs in the past or have even just glanced at the exercise books at your local bookstore or watched any number of exercise shows on TV, one thing about the Joey D. Dozen will jump out at you: it's probably the least sexy full-body workout ever. I am not throwing a lot of glitz and false promises at you. I am not claiming that you'll lose all of your unwanted fat, drop three pants sizes, or develop superhero-like strength. You're not going to lose thirty pounds in thirty days, be able to show off chiseled twelve-pack abs, or finally become the sex panther that your partner has always wanted you to be. Sorry.

If you do the exercises in the Joey D. Dozen, though, you will make your body more fit—from a biomechanical standpoint—to play golf. (You're on your own about becoming a sex panther.) I've been a bodybuilder. I've thrown around more than my share of heavy weights. This is not about building the "Look at me!" muscles such as the pecs, the biceps, and triceps. That's not what the golf swing is all about.

The golf swing is like a really good movie. It's generally not about the big-name marquee actors or actresses. What makes it work is the supporting cast. On the golf course, the big-name marquee muscles aren't really behind the perfect swing. It's the smaller, supporting muscles that ultimately decide the

When you grow up around sports, you always see people doing bench presses and a lot of other power movements, which are good for certain athletes. But doing these more golf-specific exercises makes you feel like you're training the right way. You're getting the most out of the workout because what you're doing is golf-specific. It carries over a lot easier. A lot of this stuff was new to me when I first started training, and Joey kind of opened my mind to different exercises and different avenues I could take to get better as a golfer.

—*Jason Dufner, touring professional*

You have to constantly be preparing yourself, because if you aren't, there's another guy standing right over there who is. With Joey, I know I'm going to be as prepared as possible to play. Everything we do is built around the golf swing. I'm never sore. I'm never tight. I'm the strongest I've ever been. And I got my first victory.

—*Pat Perez, touring professional*

fate of your swing and of your ball. Strengthening them properly is what's going to make your body better at swinging a club.

You won't need a lot of equipment to take on the Joey D. Dozen. All it takes is a set of resistance bands, a stability ball, a medicine ball, and a golf club. I recommend the GolfGym PowerBandz. These are special resistance bands that I personally designed to be used by professional golfers. There are generic bands out there, but honestly, I don't think they offer the design or functionality required for a golf-specific workout protocol. If you're having trouble finding any of the bands, balls, or other things you need for the program, check out the appendix at the end of the book. It'll let you know where you can find everything that you'll need.

1—STANDING HORIZONTAL ROW WITH BANDS

I'll ease you into the workout with a move that might be familiar to some of you. This standing row primarily targets the latissimus dorsi, the large muscles of the back. Your lats are the winglike muscles that, when highly developed, give a V-shaped look to the back. We're not working them to get that cobra's-head-looking back, though. Strengthening the big muscles of the back will help you keep your posture strong. I've already mentioned how we live a lifestyle that lends itself to bad posture. We sit around a lot. We hunch over our computer keyboards. And even if we do go to the gym, a lot of us focus more on pushing exercises that work the chest than on pulling exercises that work the back. This results in an imbalance that can lead to a forward-leaning posture. Poor posture can be trouble enough in your daily life. It can make you look older than you are and can be a major contributing factor to lower-back problems. On the golf course, it can cause even more problems. Poor posture will thwart any plans you have maintaining the proper spine angle.

The pulling motion that you'll do here is a great way to straighten up your back and make sure your posture stays strong. What I also like about this exer-

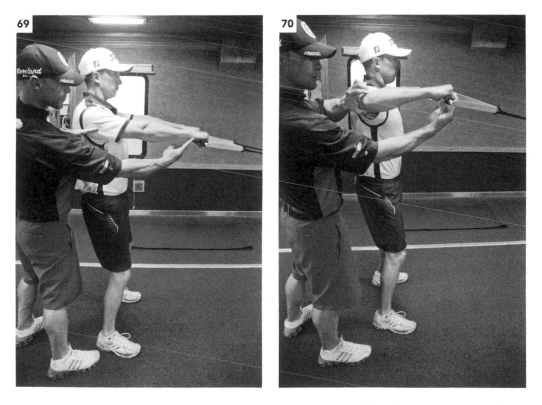

cise is that since you're doing it standing up and using bands, your core gets a workout as well. Your lower back and abs have to work to keep you standing upright. Having a stronger back and a stronger core means that you'll have the strength to get into proper golf posture at address and maintain a perfect spine angle throughout your swing.

How to do it   Anchor the bands to a solid object at around chest level. Stand facing the anchor point with feet shoulders' width apart and a band handle in each hand. Raise your arms straight up in front of you at shoulder height with your palms facing down. You should look like a sleepwalker, like a mummy from an old horror movie, or like Tim Wilkinson in Picture 69. It's your choice. There should be adequate tension in the bands before you start. If the bands are hanging limply between you and the anchor point, you might as well not be using them.

Keeping your forearms parallel to the floor, draw your elbows back until they are level with your shoulders. See Picture 70. Hold for a beat, then slowly return to the starting position to complete the rep.

11—ALTERNATING EXTERNAL SHOULDER ROTATION WITH BANDS

I can't say enough about how important healthy rotators are for your golf swing. If you didn't read my ode to the rotator cuff in chapter 6, I urge you to check it out. It's powerful stuff. In fact, I'm currently in negotiations with a top Broadway producer who wants to turn the chapter into a musical.

As a quick recap, if you can't get your arms to externally rotate to a sufficient degree at the top of your backswing, your body is going to compensate by lifting your arms into place—not rotating them into place. This lifting is usually done by leaning forward toward your target. When you lean forward, you end up in a reverse pivot, and the odds are that when you swing, you won't be able to square your clubface at impact.

On the other end of the swing, your inability to externally rotate your arms during your follow-through means that you're probably going to decelerate early to maintain your balance. This means less clubhead speed at impact, and that means less distance on your shot.

Even though this move may look similar to the horizontal row, the muscles that are actually working against the resistance of the bands in this exercise are much smaller and less powerful than your lats. Your lats are huge compared to the small muscles that externally rotate the shoulder. As a result, you want to make sure that the bands are not as taut as they were in the first exercise of the Joey D. Dozen. You want some resistance—just enough to make performing the movement a challenge.

How to do it Anchor the bands to a solid object at shoulder level. Stand facing the anchor point with feet shoulders' width apart and a band handle in each hand. Your arms should be raised to shoulder height and parallel to the ground and your elbows should be flexed at ninety degrees so that your forearms are pointed toward the anchor point. Your palms should be facing down. See Picture 71.

Slowly—and I stress *slowly*; this is not an explosive motion—rotate your right forearm up while keeping the upper part of your right arm in place. There should be a lot of right angles going on. Your upper arm should be at a ninety-degree angle to your body and parallel to the floor. Your forearm should be at a ninety-degree angle to your upper arm and perpendicular to the floor. Your palm should now be facing the anchor point. See Picture 72. Hold for a beat, then slowly return to the starting position.

Now, do the same thing with your left arm. See Picture 73. Hold for a beat, then return to the starting position to complete the rep. You may find one side does the movement easier than the other side. That's perfectly normal. If you're having trouble doing the exercise with one side or the other, simply take half a step toward the anchor point to reduce some of the resistance.

III—TWO-ARM EXTERNAL SHOULDER ROTATION WITH BANDS

Because you're doing this exercise with both hands at the same time, you're going to force your core to work a little bit harder to stabilize your body. Stronger abs and a stronger lower back will help you maintain golf posture throughout your swing and throughout your entire round. Not a bad bonus.

The core work, though, is still just the bonus. The real work is being done by the external rotators in your shoulders. Again, being able to rotate your arms sufficiently at the top of your backswing and during your follow-through will help you fine-tune your accuracy and help add distance to your game.

How to do it
Anchor the bands to a solid object at shoulder level. Stand facing the anchor point with feet shoulders' width apart and a band handle in each hand. Your arms should be raised to shoulder height and parallel to the ground, and your elbows should be flexed at ninety degrees so that your forearms are pointed toward the anchor point. Your palms should be facing down. See Picture 74.

Slowly—again, this is not an explosive motion—rotate both forearms up until they are perpendicular to the ground and your palms are facing the anchor point. Your upper arms should not move during the motion. They should remain parallel to the ground and out to your sides at shoulder height. See Picture 75. Hold for a beat, then slowly reverse the motion to complete the rep.

The Joey D. Dozen

IV—SHOULDER PROTRACTION/RETRACTION WITH BANDS

I could nag you as if I were your mother or one of your old grade-school teachers and tell you to sit up straight. Odds are you'd be able to do it for a while, but eventually you'd go back to that slouching position that you've grown accustomed to. It's not a reflection on you. Just as with most of the issues that we're dealing with in this book, it's more a reflection of what your body is capable, and not capable, of doing. One thing responsible for poor posture is weakness in the muscles of the back. (The two other primary reasons for poor posture are tightness in the muscles in the front of the body and, of course, voodoo.)

One of the lesser-worked muscle groups when it comes to fitness programs are the rhomboids. Your rhomboid major and rhomboid minor are in the center of your middle and upper back. It's their job to retract—or draw back—your shoulder blades. Weakness in the rhomboids leads to a slouching, forward-pitched C-shaped posture. That C-shape is actually just the way your body holds itself when your shoulders are protracted—or in a forward position.

Start with light resistance initially, but since there's not a lot of movement in this exercise, you can go a little heavier with the resistance from the bands. Of course, make sure you can do the movement correctly before you decide to increase the resistance. If the greater resistance is forcing you out of proper form, it's not really doing anyone any favors.

How to do it Anchor the bands to a solid object at chest level. Stand facing the anchor point with feet shoulders' width apart and a band handle in each hand. Raise your arms straight up in front of you at chest height with your palms facing each other. Keeping your posture strong and without leaning forward, lengthen your arms towards the anchor point. Imagine that you're being pulled toward the anchor point, but that your upper body isn't allowed to move—only your arms. Or, imagine that you're trying to grow a shark's fin out of your back. Either way, I want you to feel a stretch and a pull across your upper back. To do this you'll need to make sure that there's a decent amount of resistance in the bands. Your shoulders are now protracted or in a forward position. See Jason Gore in Picture 76.

Hold this position for a beat and now bring your shoulders into a retracted state by squeezing your shoulders together in back of you. Imagine you're trying to crush a walnut between your shoulder blades. The key is to keep your arms straight and not flex at the elbows. You also don't want to lean backward. See Picture 77. Hold for a beat, then lengthen your arms back into protraction to complete the rep.

V—RETRACTION WITH ALTERNATING SIDE ROTATION

It's one thing to be able to use the muscles in your back to maintain a strong posture while standing straight up and not moving—as you did in the previous exercise. You now have all the tools you'll need to be a successful mannequin. Life—and, more important, golf—requires you to be able to maintain a good posture while moving. A lot of players can look real sharp and picture-perfect at address, but once they start their takeaway, the wheels fall off. Again, it's not a reflection on the player; it's a reflection on the player's body. The body isn't strong enough in certain ways to be able to go through the required rotations without losing its posture.

With this exercise, you'll not only have to be aware of maintaining that shoulder-retracted posture in a static position, you'll have to be aware of maintaining it while rotating. In addition, you'll work on the ability to generate power. You're starting from a static position, then explode into a dynamic rotation—just as you do every time you swing a golf club.

How to do it   Anchor the bands to a solid object at chest level. Stand facing the anchor point with feet shoulders' width apart while holding the band handles with both hands. Raise your arms straight up in front of you at chest height. Keeping your posture strong and without leaning forward, lengthen your arms toward the anchor point. There should be a sufficient amount of resistance in the bands so that you feel a stretch across your back.

Keeping your arms straight and without leaning back, retract your shoulders by squeezing your shoulder blades together in back of you. Pretend I put a golf ball between your shoulder blades and told you that if you dropped it, you'd have to do all of my yard work, clean my pool, and detail my car. See Picture 78.

With your shoulder blades drawn back and without dropping the imaginary golf ball, rotate your upper body to the right. See Picture 79.

Rotate back until you're once again facing the anchor point. Maintain that squeeze between your shoulder blades. See Picture 80. Now rotate to the left. And don't drop that golf ball! See Picture 81.

Return to facing the anchor point and let your arms lengthen toward the anchor point. You should once again feel a nice pull across your upper back. That's one rep.

VI—RETRACTION WITH CONTINUOUS TWO-SIDED ROTATION

Even though this exercise seems similar to the previous one, there are some important differences. In the previous drill, you started from a still position, you twisted, then you returned to a still position. In addition to all of the postural benefits that result from maintaining good posture while rotating, it also worked on generating explosive power. You started from a static position, then burst into action.

Here, you're in continuous motion. You still have to be aware of maintaining your posture through each rotation, but now each rotation is roughly 180 degrees from beginning to end. You don't have the luxury of simply having to create and control a smaller 90-degree rotation. Now you're creating and controlling large, full-body twists. This is the indoor, and slightly controlled, version of seeing how well you can create and control movement. Successfully creating and controlling movement, as opposed to creating and then trying to control chaos, means that you can maintain good posture and a solid base throughout the exercise.

If you find yourself unable to keep your posture strong and your shoulders retracted, or if you find yourself falling all over the place, slow down your rotations or reduce the resistance slightly. You don't want to sacrifice the quality of your work. It's far better to do things correctly at a slower pace and with less resistance, than it is to do something with bad form and improper technique at a faster pace and with too much resistance.

Because it's a continuous movement with a rather large motion with resistance, it'll probably get your heart rate up a bit. That's a good thing. Your heart and lungs—just like the rest of the body parts we're dealing with—get stronger when they're forced to work harder. While golf doesn't require a lot of cardiovascular endurance, a healthy heart and healthy lungs generally lead to a longer life expectancy. If you live longer, you'll get to play more golf.

How to do it   Anchor the bands to a solid object at chest level. Stand facing the anchor point with feet shoulders' width apart while holding the band handles with both hands. Raise your arms straight up in front of you at chest height. Keeping your posture strong and without leaning forward, lengthen your arms toward the anchor point. There should be enough resistance in the bands for you to feel a stretch across your back.

Bring your shoulders into retraction by squeezing your shoulder blades together. Make sure that your arms are straight and that you aren't bending at the elbows. Rotate your body fully to the right, then fully to the left. To get as much rotation as possible, come up on the ball of the foot on the opposite side that you're rotating toward. Once to the right and once to the left completes one rep. If you find yourself unable to maintain your balance, slow down your movement or take a step or two toward the anchor point to lessen the resistance slightly. Check out Pat Perez doing this in Pictures 82 through 86. If you cut out the pictures, stapled them together along the side, and flipped quickly through them, it'd be as if you were right here in the trailer with us.

VII—BACKSWING THROUGH IMPACT WITH BANDS

Just about every movement in sports—and plenty of them in your day-to-day life—involve dynamic movement around the hips. A lot of people, including athletes, don't really do a heck of a lot to train their hips properly. They may jog, run, or bike, but while those exercises involve motion at the hips, they don't require much rotation or coordination in the hips. Think of those motions. All they require is for the legs to move from front to back.

Our hips are capable of doing much more than that. In addition to moving your legs front and back, they can raise your legs out to the side. They can also rotate the legs. Stand up for a second, press the ball of your foot into the floor, and shift your heel from side to side as if you were squashing a bug or stamping out a cigarette. That's your hip rotating your leg.

On the golf course, if you're unable to get your hips into your swing correctly, you're going to run into problems. If you can't get them to fire at the right time, your swing is going to be off and your accuracy will be off. If you can't figure out how to use them at all, you're going to become an arms-y player and you'll suffer all sorts of power issues.

Not only do you need to have strong and loose hips, but you also have to be able to use them the way you want. The golf swing can be very unforgiving. If things don't happen at the precise time they're supposed to happen, all bets are off. Few people have been successful in this sport with a swing that's 90 percent correct.

This exercise is a great way to strengthen the hips and to hardwire into your system exactly how and when they should be working in your golf swing.

How to do it   Anchor the bands to a solid object at between waist and chest height. Stand with your right side to the anchor point, so that your right ear is facing it. Hold a single band handle with both hands—as if it were a golf club—and assume a modified top-of-backswing position. Your hands should be just below shoulder height, and you should have your upper body rotated slightly while maintaining a proper spine angle. See John Rollins in Picture 87.

Just as if you were on the golf course, start your downswing with your hips. Since you aren't on the course and are holding something that is clearly not a golf club, your body may want to compensate and do the motion simply by using your arms and some upper-body rotation. The key here, though, is to get the hips involved. Look at John's right knee in Picture 88. It's starting to rotate inward. That's showing that he's using his hip to drive the motion.

Continue the swing through impact and into a shortened follow-through. Again, make sure that it's the hips that are generating the power. Look at the pivot in John's right foot in Picture 89. If he had done an arms-y swing, his right foot would still be flat on the floor.

To strengthen the hips in a balanced manner, make sure that you also do this exercise from your weak side.

89

VIII—ADDRESS THROUGH IMPACT WITH RELOAD

The hips not only have to know when they need to create movement during your swing, they also have to know when they need to control movement during your swing. The hips are great generators of power, but they're also incredible stabilizers. People just don't give their hips enough credit!

In this exercise, you're going to use your hips as both stabilizers and power generators. During takeaway and up to the top of the backswing, the hips need to stabilize your body while your upper body and arms rotate into proper position.

Just as in the previous exercise, you need to have complete control over your hips if you really want to get the most out of your game and the most out of your swing. Again, because you're not out on the course and you're not actually holding a club, you may tend to treat this like any other exercise you may ever have done in the gym and try to muscle your way through by using some of the more familiar "gym muscles." To prevent that, you have to concentrate on what your hips are doing. Whether they're letting the rest of your body do what it needs to do during takeaway, or generating the maximum power at impact, you need to make your hips the focal point of this movement. In a perfect world, you'd get to spend your time focusing on the hips of members of the opposite sex, but this is just one of the many sacrifices that you'll make for the sake of your golf game.

How to do it   Anchor the bands to a solid object at between waist and chest height. Stand with your left side to the anchor point, so that your left ear is facing it. Hold a single band handle with both hands—as if it were a golf club—and assume a slightly tweaked address position. Your spine angle should be strong and your arms should be about forty-five degrees forward—toward your target—of where your ball would be. There should be light resistance in the band. See John Rollins in Picture 90.

Rotate back into a modified version of your backswing, bringing your hands up to about shoulder height. Everything else should be done exactly the way you would do it on the course. Maintain proper spine angle through your rotation, and keep your head position strong. At the top of the move, you should be able to look straight down and see your left shoulder. See Picture 91. Again be aware of how your hips are stabilizing your body through the movement.

Here's where things get interesting. To show you how different it feels when your hips are involved in your downswing versus how it feels when they aren't, you're first going to do your downswing with your hips remaining neutral and still in stabilization mode. Rotate your body down toward impact, but keep your hips square to your ball. Stop just shy of impact—at about the point when your hands are at the top of your right thigh. See Picture 92.

Now rotate back into that same modified backswing. Again, maintain a good spine angle and head position. See Picture 93.

Finally, take your swing through downswing and impact using your hips to drive the motion. See Picture 94. It should feel as different as night and day when compared to the first downswing you'd done. The idea is to get you to understand just how important it is to properly use your hips to generate power. This hip-driven swing is going to give you more consistency and more power on the course.

Just as before, to train the hips in a balanced way, make sure you do this drill from your weak side as well.

IX—SIMULATED SWING WITH STABILITY BALL

This is a surprisingly good way to work on your stabilization, balance, and flexibility. There's even some strengthening going on. Not a bad payoff for a drill that just uses a giant ball. Having to deal with something that's so much larger and significantly less user-friendly than your golf club is going to force your body to work a little harder than usual. Initially, you may find it a bit tougher to keep your feet under you. That's a good thing. It's one of the reasons I'm having you do this exercise. The more you can get your body to maintain its balance and be able to stabilize itself in increasingly oddball situations, the better. You'll find your lower body getting less and less affected by the awkwardness of swinging with the stability ball—and that's bankable proof that your balance is improving and that the stabilizers in your lower body are getting better at doing their job.

As far as upper-body adaptations go, because the ball is about a zillion times wider than your club, you'll be developing more range of motion around the shoulders with your arms. This is because when holding the ball, your hands are about three feet apart—as opposed to being next to each other when you're holding your club. If you get a chance, grab your stability ball and a golf club and find a mirror. Compare your backswing while holding the ball with your backswing while holding your club. If you're right-handed, your right arm only rotates up and back as high as your left arm will allow it to. When swinging with the ball, though, when your left arm has rotated as far back as it goes, it forces your right arm to rotate even farther back. What that's doing is giving your pecs—the muscles in your chest—a nice stretch that they wouldn't have got otherwise.

In addition to being stretched and lengthened, your pecs also get some strengthening. Your chest muscles allow you to squeeze the ball and hang on to it throughout your swing. If your pecs weren't strong enough, every time you attempted to swing with the ball, it would fly across the room and everyone would become annoyed with you.

How to do it   Assume your regular address position with strong golf posture and proper spine angle. Go through your regular swing doing everything you'd do if you were out on the golf course. Keep your eye on where your ball would be, maintain your spine angle, fire your hips at the proper time, etc. Oh, yeah—and use a giant ball instead of a club. Check out Ryuji Imada doing it in Pictures 95 and 96.

I also want you to swing from the opposite side while holding the stability ball. This will help balance out your training to make sure that you're developing stability and flexibility equally for both your right and left sides. It'll also give you more confidence in your abilities. You may never actually have to play from your weaker side, but at least now you know that, in a pinch, you'd be able to comfortably swing a giant inflatable ball from your weaker side.

X—PELVIC TILT IN GOLF POSTURE WITH STABILITY BALL

As I mentioned in the prescription chapter for pelvic tilt and posture, figuring out how to move your pelvis might be one of the tougher things that my program asks of you. For some, it'll come naturally. For others, it's a movement that they've never been asked to do—and if you've gone thirty, forty, fifty, or more years without ever having done something, figuring out how to do it can take some time.

That said, it's worth putting in the time to get it down. There's no quicker way to straighten your posture than by tilting your pelvis forward. The motion creates a chain reaction that—combined with all of the other strengthening you're doing—forces your upper body into perfect posture. Again, a lot of times, you may think that you're in good golf posture because your shoulders are, theoretically, where they're supposed to be at address. Often, though, while your shoulders may be in the right place, they got there not because you have good golf posture, but because you've rounded your back.

Trying to swing a club with bad posture is not only not good for your back, it's also not good for your golf game. With a rounded back, it's virtually impossible to get a true spine rotation when you swing. You're taken out of plane the moment you start your takeaway. The result is a completely unpredictable swing with completely unpredictable results. You may end up hitting the ball where you want it go, but it would be more a result of good luck than good technique.

This version of the pelvic tilt exercise is a little more user-friendly than the one I had you do during the assessment. With the ball behind your lower back, it gives you more of a feel for what's supposed to be moving. If you can get the ball to move slightly while preventing your legs and upper body from moving, you're on the right track.

How to do it   Stand at address with a stability ball between you and a wall. The ball should be right at the base of your tailbone. Slowly round your back and tilt your pelvis back. This will kick your hips down and forward slightly. See Tim Wilkinson demonstrating a slightly C-shaped posture in Picture 97.

To get to the other extreme of pelvic positioning, tilt your pelvis forward. This will kick your hips backward slightly and, if you're doing it properly, will automatically correct your rounded back and spine. See Picture 98. Again, you may find this difficult to do at first. Unless you've had training as a belly dancer, you've probably never been asked to do this before. As I've pointed out, though, the stronger you are through the pelvis and hips and the more you are in control of your pelvis and hips, the better able you'll be to maintain good posture throughout the swing, and the better able you'll be to time the firing of the hip muscles to maximize power at impact.

Tilting your pelvis backward and then forward equals one rep.

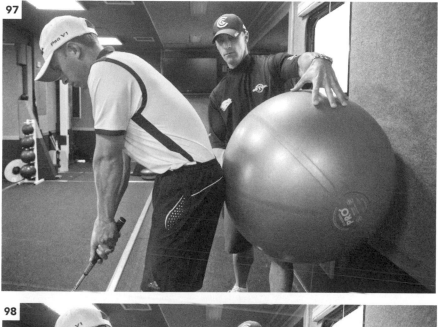

XI—SEATED ROTATION IN GOLF POSTURE ON STABILITY BALL

As with most of the exercises in the Joey D. Dozen, there's a lot of added value in this one. While it may look, and initially feel, like the assessment you did to check your upper-body rotation, there's more to it than first meets the eye.

First, doing this drill will improve your ability to rotate your upper body. You're using the momentum you create during the rotation as well as the weight of a medicine ball to assist you and ease you gently into a deeper rotation. If you were moving in slow motion, you wouldn't be getting that same assistance. If you were using a balloon and not an eight-pound ball, you wouldn't be getting that same assistance. The combination of the speed of the movement and the weight of the ball—extended as far as possible from your body—is what you can thank for those few extra degrees of rotation that you'll take home from this.

You're also strengthening your lower, middle, and upper back. Since you have to maintain golf posture throughout this entire drill, you are forcing the muscles in your back—the ones that are responsible for keeping your spine angle correct—to work.

Finally, you're strengthening your lower body and making it better at being able to stabilize you. As I said, this may feel a lot like the assessment test you did, but that test was done with the ball against a wall. There's a big difference when you take the ball away from the wall. Now, it's your lower body that has to keep it in place. And you have to keep it in place because, well, you're sitting on it, and if it decides to roll to the other side of the room, you're going to end up on the floor.

How to do it   Sit on a stability ball holding a medicine ball between your hands. Assume proper golf posture. See Travis Perkins in Picture 99. Rotate your arms up and back to the right while maintaining good golf posture. Consider it a slightly less extreme version of your backswing with your arms only coming up as high as your shoulders. Keep both feet flat on the floor and your head from moving. Your eyes should be trained on where your ball would be. See Picture 100.

Rotate back to the starting position, then rotate to the left. Again, keep your feet flat on the floor and your gaze fixed on your imaginary ball. See Picture 101. Once to the right, then once to the left, equals one rep.

101

XII—SQUAT AND OVERHEAD ARM-RAISE

First, this is a slightly more difficult version of the squat and overhead arm-raise that you did during the assessment. If you had trouble with it during the assessment and are currently working on the full-body strength and coordination prescription exercises, I want you to do the assessment version of this exercise for now. Let the combination of those prescription drills you're doing and the assistance of the stability ball from the assessment version slowly ease you into this slightly more challenging take on the movement. Eventually, you will be doing this version of the exercise. I guarantee it.

Whether you're doing this version or the assessment version, expect a whole bunch of benefits. Few body parts aren't called into play in this exercise, and that's a really good thing. The golf swing uses just about every muscle and involves movement around just about every joint in the body. The more you can work on that coordinated integration of body parts, the better.

Strengthening your quads and glutes with the squat portion of this exercise will do a few things for you on the golf course. It'll give you the lower-body strength you need to stabilize yourself throughout your swing. This movement will also lead to greater range of motion around the knees and the hips, which will allow you to be in a better position at address. You won't be as stiff-legged and you won't be forced into a straight-up position. The closer you can get to dropping down to where your knees are flexed at ninety degrees and your thighs are parallel to the ground, the more comfortable you'll be at setup and address.

North of your hips, being able to raise the club directly overhead will keep your chest and shoulders open, which will lead to better posture on and off the golf course. On the course, as I've said throughout this book, a strong posture will allow you to maintain the proper spine angle and remain on plane throughout your swing. You can't ask for more than that. Off the course, strong posture will make you appear a little bit taller, help you breathe more easily, and work to combat lower-back pain. Again, you can't ask for more than that.

How to do it   Start in address. See Ryuji Imada in Picture 102.

Without losing golf posture, bring the club up so that you can grab it with both hands. The club should be parallel to the ground at midthigh level. Your hands should be slightly wider than shoulders' width apart. See Picture 103.

Again, without losing golf posture, raise your arms above your head so that your biceps are behind your ears. Your arms should be straight, with no bend at the elbows. See Picture 104.

Slowly, drop into a squat by kicking your hips back and bending at the knees as Ryuji is doing in Picture 105. In this position, your lower legs should

be perpendicular to the floor and your thighs should be parallel to the floor. Your knees should be aligned over your feet.

That is the Joey D. Dozen—twelve moves that anyone who has the slightest desire to play golf to the best of his ability should be doing. Every one of those movements has been designed to get your body in the optimal condition it needs to be from a biomechanical standpoint. I'll repeat—it's not the sexiest of workouts out there. Heck, when the heaviest dumbbell you're going to play with weighs just five pounds, you know that this isn't a fitness program that will make you want to cut the sleeves off all of your shirts.

Coupled with the prescription exercises you're doing, these twelve exercises will get your body in the shape it needs to be in to let you take advantage of what your swing coach or the pro at your club is teaching you to do.

This program is the most comprehensive and sport-specific protocol available for the golfer's body. These exercises and workouts have transformed the bodies and the games of some of the top players in the world, players whose livelihoods depend on how their bodies perform on the golf course.

Your livelihood probably depends on doing something else. You probably look at your time on the golf course as a break from the stresses of doing that something else. Used correctly, this program will allow you to have more fun and experience more success during those well-earned breaks.

You're about to find out how to fit all these exercises and prescriptions into your busy life.

13 Structuring Your Workouts

or . . . What Am I Supposed to Do?

Okay, so you have the science behind what this program is about, and you have the exercises that you're supposed to do. Now I'm going to tell you how to fit it all into your busy schedule. I don't expect you to be spending all sorts of time in the gym. What I'd like you to commit to is a twenty-minute workout three times a week. If you can give me an hour a week, I'm going to give you a better, more consistent, and more enjoyable golf game. Not a bad deal if you ask me.

The way I'm going to break it down for you, you'll have no more than eight different exercises to do for each workout. What you'll be doing depends on how your body fared on the assessments. This is a personalized workout based on what *your* body can and cannot do. We've all been created a little bit differently, and we all have lifestyles and histories that make us stronger, weaker, tighter, or looser than the next guy. Ryuji Imada at five feet eight inches and 150 pounds isn't Pat Perez at six feet and 200 pounds and isn't Jason Gore at six feet one inch and 235 pounds. If all those in your regular Saturday-morning foursome were on my program, it's unlikely that any of you would be doing the exact same workout. That was the whole point of the six assessments. You discovered what specific things were preventing your body from doing what it needs to do on the golf course. Now it's time to do something about them. Any program that has everyone doing the exact

> Some guys have had great results with him who had no athletic background whatsoever. And that's the thing about Joey. You don't have to be an athlete to do these things. They're simple maneuvers and moves that if you're coordinated enough to swing a golf club, then you're coordinated enough to do things he wants you to do.
> —*Travis Perkins, touring professional*

> Here I am at forty-nine. I play a lot of tournaments. I practice a lot. I haven't had any injuries. And my game has gotten better in the last eight or nine years. Working with Joey has enabled me to stay conditioned, keep my flexibility, strength, and speed up, so that I can compete with twenty-year-old guys.
>
> —Tom Pernice Jr., touring professional

same thing without factoring in an individual's strengths and weaknesses can't be as effective as it could be. I'm not about cookie-cutter, one-size-fits-all workouts.

I'll explain exactly how I want you to use the program based on the results of your assessments. It's the same thing that I do for my players. I'll even give you some sample four-week breakdowns that go through the workouts—exercise by exercise—so you'll understand precisely how I expect you to go about fixing your body. I assume that after a month of my hand-holding, you'll be able to figure out the exercise and workout pattern on your own. Heck, if you've made it to chapter 13 in this book, you have to be a pretty intelligent person.

I don't want you to go from spending no time working on these issues to spending an hour a day working on them. These muscle groups and body parts didn't become weak or tight overnight. Getting them back to the way they should be is going to take some time. You'll notice results quickly, but if you overdo it too early, the only thing you're going to notice is discomfort and maybe an injury that may end up sidetracking you and your progress. The assessments show that your body has been doing something slightly out of whack for a long time. You can't fix it in an hour. The things that we're dealing with—movement around the shoulders and hips and rotation around the spine—all involve small muscles. They've thrown up a red flag during our assessments because, over time, they've either not been used enough due to day-to-day movement patterns or they've been sabotaged by other muscles due to compensations that your body is making.

I've already pointed out that this is a personalized program. It's tailored exactly to the needs of your body. It's doubtful that your workout will be the same as anyone else's. Just as exciting is that because of the way things are structured, even within your own program it's doubtful that any two of your workouts will ever be the same. The personalization and customization let us cover a lot of ground—without that ground ever becoming boring or routine. People give up on fitness programs mainly because they become bored with them. Varying what you do when you work out will keep things fresh. Of course, seeing what the program is doing to your golf game should also keep you motivated.

Remember, because you're going to be assessing yourself every three months, the prescriptions will be changing. This will at all times ensure that the workout you're doing is the precise one that's going to keep your body healthy and happy. That's going to mean more fun both on and off the course.

Here are the basic rules.

> Travel is very hard on our bodies. Maintenance and training are important if I want to have a long career in this business.
>
> —*Ryuji Imada, touring professional*

If you have two or fewer prescriptions to take care of, then you're going to be doing them with the Joey D. Dozen split into two sections. If you have three or four prescriptions, then you'll be doing them with the Joey D. Dozen divided into three sections. And if you had five or six assessments that gave you trouble, don't worry. I have you covered. You'll be doing them with the Joey D. Dozen broken up into four sections.

Every workout will be made up of eight exercises. Depending on how you did during the assessments, it means you'll do three, four, or six exercises from the Joey D. Dozen. The rest will be prescription exercises focused on taking care of your specific issues. Over the next few pages I give three different workout scenarios and schedules that represent three workouts per week for four weeks. You can see that after I map out what I want you to do from the Joey D. Dozen, I then simply cycle through the prescription exercises in the order they're listed in that particular prescription's chapter. Please use these sample programs as the template for your own program.

Here's what you're about to see. Scenario One is for a person with two prescriptions. It can also be used by someone with just a single prescription. Each workout will involve six exercises from the Joey D. Dozen and two prescription exercises. The Joey D. Dozen exercises are split like this . . .

Standing Horizontal Row with Bands
Alternating External Shoulder Rotation with Bands
Retraction with Continuous Two-Sided Rotation
Simulated Swing with Stability Ball
Pelvic Tilt in Golf Posture with Stability Ball
Squat and Overhead Arm-Raise

Two-Arm External Shoulder Rotation with Bands
Shoulder Protraction/Retraction with Bands

Retraction with Alternating Side Rotation
Backswing Through Impact with Bands
Address Through Impact with Reload
Seated Rotation in Golf Posture on Stability Ball

Scenario Two is for a golfer with four prescriptions. It can also be used for someone with three prescriptions. The Joey D. Dozen gets broken down here like this . . .

Standing Horizontal Row with Bands
Shoulder Protraction/Retraction with Bands
Backswing Through Impact with Bands
Address Through Impact with Reload

Alternating External Shoulder Rotation with Bands
Retraction with Continuous Two-Sided Rotation
Simulated Swing with Stability Ball
Pelvic Tilt in Golf Posture with Stability Ball

Two-Arm External Shoulder Rotation with Bands
Retraction with Alternating Side Rotation
Seated Rotation in Golf Posture on Stability Ball
Squat and Overhead Arm-Raise

Finally, Scenario Three is for a player who has some difficulty with all six assessments, but it can serve as a template for someone with five prescriptions, as well. The Joey D. Dozen—broken into four chunks—looks like this . . .

Standing Horizontal Row with Bands
Backswing Through Impact with Bands
Address Through Impact with Reload

Alternating External Shoulder Rotation with Bands
Retraction with Continuous Two-Sided Rotation
Pelvic Tilt in Golf Posture with Stability Ball

Two-Arm External Shoulder Rotation with Bands
Retraction with Alternating Side Rotation
Seated Rotation in Golf Posture on Stability Ball

Shoulder Protraction/Retraction with Bands
Simulated Swing with Stability Ball
Squat and Overhead Arm-Raise

The only other ground rules are these . . .

All exercises will be done in sets of ten repetitions.
For the first two weeks of the program, you'll do one set of every exercise.
After the second week, you'll do two sets of every exercise.

It's time to put down the book and start fixing your body.

> The neat thing is that you're not asking people to completely change their lifestyle. It's setting them up with a program that allows them to improve their game with golf-specific biomechanical conditioning. It gives them another tool to be able to practice. And as a swing coach, that's what I'm talking about all the time—doing something in a golf-specific way even though you don't get a chance to get out to the course or the practice facility.
> —*Todd Jones, Head Instructor,*
> *PGA Tour Academy*

Scenario One

Two Prescriptions—External Shoulder Rotation and Lower Body Rotation

The prescription exercises are in bold.

Week One—Workout One

Standing Horizontal Row with Bands
Alternating External Shoulder Rotation with Bands
Retraction with Continuous Two-Sided Rotation
Simulated Swing with Stability Ball
Pelvic Tilt in Golf Posture with Stability Ball
Squat and Overhead Arm-Raise
One-Armed Row And Assisted Rotation
Hip Turn With Medicine Ball

Week One—Workout Two

Two-Arm External Shoulder Rotation with Bands
Shoulder Protraction/Retraction with Bands
Retraction with Alternating Side Rotation
Backswing Through Impact with Bands
Address Through Impact with Reload
Seated Rotation in Golf Posture on Stability Ball
Standing External Rotation
2:00 To 10:00 Rollover With Stability Ball

Week One—Workout Three

Standing Horizontal Row with Bands
Alternating External Shoulder Rotation with Bands
Retraction with Continuous Two-Sided Rotation
Simulated Swing with Stability Ball
Pelvic Tilt in Golf Posture with Stability Ball
Squat and Overhead Arm-Raise
Standing Internal Rotation
Continuous Hip Turns Over Stability Ball

Scenario One

Week Two—Workout One

Two-Arm External Shoulder Rotation with Bands
Shoulder Protraction/Retraction with Bands
Retraction with Alternating Side Rotation
Backswing Through Impact with Bands
Address Through Impact with Reload
Seated Rotation in Golf Posture on Stability Ball
Shoulder Stabilization On A Stability Ball
Hip Turn With Medicine Ball

Week Two—Workout Two

Standing Horizontal Row with Bands
Alternating External Shoulder Rotation with Bands
Retraction with Continuous Two-Sided Rotation
Simulated Swing with Stability Ball
Pelvic Tilt in Golf Posture with Stability Ball
Squat and Overhead Arm-Raise
One-Armed Row And Assisted Rotation
2:00 To 10:00 Rollover With Stability Ball

Week Two—Workout Three

Two-Arm External Shoulder Rotation with Bands
Shoulder Protraction/Retraction with Bands
Retraction with Alternating Side Rotation
Backswing Through Impact with Bands
Address Through Impact with Reload
Seated Rotation in Golf Posture on Stability Ball
Standing External Rotation
Continuous Hip Turns Over Stability Ball

Scenario One

Week Three—Workout One
Standing Horizontal Row with Bands
Alternating External Shoulder Rotation with Bands
Retraction with Continuous Two-Sided Rotation
Simulated Swing with Stability Ball
Pelvic Tilt in Golf Posture with Stability Ball
Squat and Overhead Arm-Raise
Standing Internal Rotation
Hip Turn With Medicine Ball

Week Three—Workout Two
Two-Arm External Shoulder Rotation with Bands
Shoulder Protraction/Retraction with Bands
Retraction with Alternating Side Rotation
Backswing Through Impact with Bands
Address Through Impact with Reload
Seated Rotation in Golf Posture on Stability Ball
Shoulder Stabilization On A Stability Ball
2:00 To 10:00 Rollover With Stability Ball

Week Three—Workout Three
Standing Horizontal Row with Bands
Alternating External Shoulder Rotation with Bands
Retraction with Continuous Two-Sided Rotation
Simulated Swing with Stability Ball
Pelvic Tilt in Golf Posture with Stability Ball
Squat and Overhead Arm-Raise
One-Armed Row And Assisted Rotation
Continuous Hip Turns Over Stability Ball

Scenario One

Week Four—Workout One
Two-Arm External Shoulder Rotation with Bands
Shoulder Protraction/Retraction with Bands
Retraction with Alternating Side Rotation
Backswing Through Impact with Bands
Address Through Impact with Reload
Seated Rotation in Golf Posture on Stability Ball
Standing External Rotation
Hip Turn With Medicine Ball

Week Four—Workout Two
Standing Horizontal Row with Bands
Alternating External Shoulder Rotation with Bands
Retraction with Continuous Two-Sided Rotation
Simulated Swing with Stability Ball
Pelvic Tilt in Golf Posture with Stability Ball
Squat and Overhead Arm-Raise
Standing Internal Rotation
2:00 To 10:00 Rollover With Stability Ball

Week Four—Workout Three
Two-Arm External Shoulder Rotation with Bands
Shoulder Protraction/Retraction with Bands
Retraction with Alternating Side Rotation
Backswing Through Impact with Bands
Address Through Impact with Reload
Seated Rotation in Golf Posture on Stability Ball
Shoulder Stabilization On A Stability Ball
Continuous Hip Turns Over Stability Ball

Scenario Two

Four Prescriptions—Upper Body Rotation, Lower Body Rotation, Pelvic Tilt, and Balance

The prescription exercises are in bold.

Week One—Workout One

Standing Horizontal Row with Bands
Shoulder Protraction/Retraction with Bands
Backswing Through Impact with Bands
Address Through Impact with Reload
Address To Backswing With Medicine Ball
Hip Turn With Medicine Ball
Pelvic Tilt On Mat
One-Legged Golf Posture

Week One—Workout Two

Alternating External Shoulder Rotation with Bands
Retraction with Continuous Two-Sided Rotation
Simulated Swing with Stability Ball
Pelvic Tilt in Golf Posture with Stability Ball
Impact To Follow-Through With Medicine Ball
2:00 To 10:00 Rollover With Stability Ball
Hip Drop On Stability Ball
One-Legged Address To Takeaway

Week One—Workout Three

Two-Arm External Shoulder Rotation with Bands
Retraction with Alternating Side Rotation
Seated Rotation in Golf Posture on Stability Ball
Squat and Overhead Arm-Raise
One-Armed Address To Backswing With Bands
Continuous Hip Turns Over Stability Ball
Pelvic Dip On Stability Ball
One-Legged Impact To Follow-Through

Scenario Two

Week Two—Workout One

Standing Horizontal Row with Bands
Shoulder Protraction/Retraction with Bands
Backswing Through Impact with Bands
Address Through Impact with Reload
One-Armed Impact To Follow-Through With Bands
Hip Turn With Medicine Ball
Pelvic Tilt On Mat
One-Legged Chest Opener

Week Two—Workout Two

Alternating External Shoulder Rotation with Bands
Retraction with Continuous Two-Sided Rotation
Simulated Swing with Stability Ball
Pelvic Tilt in Golf Posture with Stability Ball
Address To Backswing With Medicine Ball
2:00 To 10:00 Rollover With Stability Ball
Hip Drop On Stability Ball
One-Legged Golf Posture

Week Two—Workout Three

Two-Arm External Shoulder Rotation with Bands
Retraction with Alternating Side Rotation
Seated Rotation in Golf Posture on Stability Ball
Squat and Overhead Arm-Raise
Impact To Follow-Through With Medicine Ball
Continuous Hip Turns Over Stability Ball
Pelvic Dip On Stability Ball
One-Legged Address To Takeaway

Scenario Two

Week Three—Workout One
Standing Horizontal Row with Bands
Shoulder Protraction/Retraction with Bands
Backswing Through Impact with Bands
Address Through Impact with Reload
One-Armed Address To Backswing With Bands
Hip Turn With Medicine Ball
Pelvic Tilt On Mat
One-Legged Impact To Follow-Through

Week Three—Workout Two
Alternating External Shoulder Rotation with Bands
Retraction with Continuous Two-Sided Rotation
Simulated Swing with Stability Ball
Pelvic Tilt in Golf Posture with Stability Ball
One-Armed Impact To Follow-Through With Bands
2:00 To 10:00 Rollover With Stability Ball
Hip Drop On Stability Ball
One-Legged Chest Opener

Week Three—Workout Three
Two-Arm External Shoulder Rotation with Bands
Retraction with Alternating Side Rotation
Seated Rotation in Golf Posture on Stability Ball
Squat and Overhead Arm-Raise
Address To Backswing With Medicine Ball
Continuous Hip Turns Over Stability Ball
Pelvic Dip On Stability Ball
One-Legged Golf Posture

Scenario Two

Week Four—Workout One
Standing Horizontal Row with Bands
Shoulder Protraction/Retraction with Bands
Backswing Through Impact with Bands
Address Through Impact with Reload
Impact To Follow-Through With Medicine Ball
Hip Turn With Medicine Ball
Pelvic Tilt On Mat
One-Legged Address To Takeaway

Week Four—Workout Two
Alternating External Shoulder Rotation with Bands
Retraction with Continuous Two-Sided Rotation
Simulated Swing with Stability Ball
Pelvic Tilt in Golf Posture with Stability Ball
One-Armed Address To Backswing With Bands
2:00 To 10:00 Rollover With Stability Ball
Hip Drop On Stability Ball
One-Legged Impact To Follow-Through

Week Four—Workout Three
Two-Arm External Shoulder Rotation with Bands
Retraction with Alternating Side Rotation
Seated Rotation in Golf Posture on Stability Ball
Squat and Overhead Arm-Raise
One-Armed Impact To Follow-Through With Bands
Continuous Hip Turns Over Stability Ball
Pelvic Dip On Stability Ball
One-Legged Chest Opener

Scenario Three

All Six Prescriptions
The prescription exercises are in bold.

Week One—Workout One
Standing Horizontal Row with Bands
Backswing Through Impact with Bands
Address Through Impact with Reload
One-Armed Row And Assisted Rotation
Address To Backswing With Medicine Ball
Hip Turn With Medicine Ball
Pelvic Tilt On Mat
One-Legged Golf Posture

Week One—Workout Two
Alternating External Shoulder Rotation with
    Bands
Retraction with Continuous Two-Sided Rotation
Pelvic Tilt in Golf Posture with Stability Ball
Air Bench
Standing External Rotation
Impact To Follow-Through With Medicine
    Ball
2:00 To 10:00 Rollover With Stability Ball
Hip Drop On Stability Ball

Week One—Workout Three
Two-Arm External Shoulder Rotation with
    Bands
Retraction with Alternating Side Rotation
Seated Rotation in Golf Posture on Stability Ball
One-Legged Address To Takeaway
Seated Overhead Extension
Standing Internal Rotation
One-Armed Address To Backswing With
    Bands
Continuous Hip Turns Over Stability Ball

Scenario Three

Week Two—Workout One
Shoulder Protraction/Retraction with Bands
Simulated Swing with Stability Ball
Squat and Overhead Arm-Raise
Pelvic Dip On Stability Ball
One-Legged Impact To Follow-Through
Forward Lunge With Overhead Extension
    And Rotation
Shoulder Stabilization On A Stability Ball
One-Armed Impact To Follow-Through With
    Bands

Week Two—Workout Two
Standing Horizontal Row with Bands
Backswing Through Impact with Bands
Address Through Impact with Reload
One-Armed Impact To Follow-Through With
    Bands
Pelvic Tilt On Mat
One-Legged Chest Opener
Reverse Lunge With Overhead Extension
One-Armed Row And Assisted Rotation

Week Two—Workout Three
Alternating External Shoulder Rotation with
    Bands
Retraction with Continuous Two-Sided Rotation
Pelvic Tilt in Golf Posture with Stability Ball
Address To Backswing With Medicine Ball
2:00 To 10:00 Rollover With Stability Ball
Hip Drop On Stability Ball
One-Legged Golf Posture
Air Bench

Scenario Three

Week Three—Workout One
Two-Arm External Shoulder Rotation with
Bands
Retraction with Alternating Side Rotation
Seated Rotation in Golf Posture on Stability Ball
Standing External Rotation
**Impact To Follow-Through With Medicine
Ball**
Continuous Hip Turns Over Stability Ball
Pelvic Dip On Stability Ball
One-Legged Address To Takeaway

Week Three—Workout Two
Shoulder Protraction/Retraction with Bands
Simulated Swing with Stability Ball
Squat and Overhead Arm-Raise
Seated Overhead Extension
Standing Internal Rotation
**One-Armed Address To Backswing With
Bands**
Hip Turn With Medicine Ball
Pelvic Tilt On Mat

Week Three—Workout Three
Standing Horizontal Row with Bands
Backswing Through Impact with Bands
Address Through Impact with Reload
One-Legged Impact To Follow-Through
**Forward Lunge With Overhead Extension
And Rotation**
Shoulder Stabilization On A Stability Ball
**One-Armed Impact To Follow-Through With
Bands**
2:00 To 10:00 Rollover With Stability Ball

Scenario Three

Week Four—Workout One
Alternating External Shoulder Rotation with
Bands
Retraction with Continuous Two-Sided Rotation
Pelvic Tilt in Golf Posture with Stability Ball
Hip Drop On Stability Ball
One-Legged Chest Opener
Reverse Lunge With Overhead Extension
One-Armed Row And Assisted Rotation
Address To Backswing With Medicine Ball

Week Four—Workout Two
Two-Arm External Shoulder Rotation with
Bands
Retraction with Alternating Side Rotation
Seated Rotation in Golf Posture on Stability Ball
Continuous Hip Turns Over Stability Ball
Pelvic Dip On Stability Ball
One-Legged Golf Posture
Air Bench
Standing External Rotation

Week Four—Workout Three
Shoulder Protraction/Retraction with Bands
Simulated Swing with Stability Ball
Squat and Overhead Arm-Raise
**Impact To Follow-Through With Medicine
Ball**
Hip Turn With Medicine Ball
Pelvic Tilt On Mat
One-Legged Address To Takeaway
Seated Overhead Extension

14 Your New Golf Body

or . . . Now What?

The good news is that if you've been following the game plan—putting in your time to fix your body using my assessments and prescriptions and strengthening your body in a golf-specific way using the Joey D. Dozen—your game is going to be a lot better. Your body will now let you do all of those things that you've either always wanted to do on the golf course or that you've fooled yourself into believing you were correctly doing on the golf course.

The bad news is that if you're about to tee it up for the first time all year and it's a forty-two-degree, early-spring day, I don't care how well you prepared your body at home or in the gym, if you try to blast a 250-yard drive off the first tee, you're going to hurt yourself.

In case you haven't been paying attention and didn't pick up on it the first 11 billion times I said it, my whole program is about getting your body in the shape it needs to be in to do the things you want it to do. The exercises you've been doing are a major part of that, but they're not the whole deal. Just because your body can now, biomechanically, move the way it has to for a sound and proper swing on the course, it doesn't mean it can do it without proper preparation.

STRETCH FOR SUCCESS

The only way to get the most out of your body when you're on the course is to make sure that everything you've worked on—your muscles, joints, etc.—is ready to get busy. That means a warm-up and stretching routine that you'll do before every round you play, before every bucket of practice balls you hit, and before every chipping or putting session you put in. Just like the workouts, the stretching is golf-specific. We've all seen guys go through some halfhearted

I'd be the kind of guy who would just show up on the range and I'd do my normal club-over-the-head thing to stretch my shoulders and back and then do some rotations and turning. You know. Whatever. It was the minimal and basic types of stretches that you hear people talking about. Once I got involved with Joey and started stretching the way he stretches, it enabled me to start warming up and play and never really get tight. Everything felt very good and relaxed, and I was ready to go play the best I could.

—*John Rollins, touring professional*

stretching before they play—a few minutes of some moves that their high school baseball or football coach may have shown them twenty-five years ago. That's all well and good if you're planning on trying to go from first to third on a single to right field or nail your receiver between the numbers on a short screen pass. But if you're about to play golf, you need to be preparing your body for golf-specific motions.

Stretching doesn't have to be an elaborate ceremony. All we're doing is making sure that your body has been prepped in the correct way for it to perform optimally. If you've been sitting at your desk all day and are sneaking out for an afternoon round, or, worse, if you woke up at 5:00 a.m. and have a 6:30 a.m. tee time, your body has spent time stiffening up in a position that is decidedly not all that great for golf. That's where the Joey D. Half Dozen come in. These are six simple stretches that will make sure that you're ready to play your best and that you won't spend the next day or two eating ibuprofen and smelling all wintergreeny from the big dollops of Ben-Gay you've been massaging into your sore spots.

For a warm-up, I just want you to walk or jog around for three or four minutes. That's not asking a lot. Golf courses are beautiful places. There's grass. There are trees. Odds are that while you're golfing, someone—probably someone that you know—is sitting at his desk working. Enjoy the air. Enjoy the view. Enjoy that you're not at your desk.

Now that you're warm, it's time to stretch.

I—HIP AND KNEE FLEXION STRETCH

Wake up your body both figuratively and literally with this stretch that's based on the oddly named Good Morning strengthening exercise. I've woken up thousands of times in my life and have never done so in this fashion. In any event, this stretch will loosen the muscles in your lower back, glutes, and legs.

How to do it   Assume golf posture while holding a club parallel to the ground at midthigh level. Your hands should be slightly wider than shoulders' width apart. See the good-looking guy with the massive forearms in Picture 106.

Slowly kick back your hips and bend your knees while maintaining your spine angle. Let your arms—and the club—hang directly down from your shoulders to a slightly below-the-knee level. See Picture 107.

While maintaining a straight back, come up to a standing position. See Picture 108. Hold for a beat, then go right back into golf posture to complete the rep.

Do ten complete reps being very aware of maintaining a strong posture.

II—STANDING ROTATION

Ease into the rotational movements you'll be doing with this standing, twisting stretch. Go slow at first, and as things get looser, go a little bit deeper into every rotation.

How to do it   Stand with your feet slightly wider than shoulders' width apart while holding a golf club with both hands at chest level. Your arms should be straight out in front of you with your hands about the same distance apart as your feet. See Picture 109.

Twist to the right, keeping your arms straight and the club parallel to the ground at chest level. To get the most out of the rotation, pivot your left foot and go up on the ball of the foot. See Picture 110. Return to a center-facing position, pause for a beat, then twist your upper body to the left. Again, to maximize rotation, pivot your right foot and go up on the ball of the foot. See Picture 111.

Do ten twists in each direction.

III—STANDING ROTATION IN GOLF POSTURE

Now that you're getting loose, you'll take the rotational move in a more golf-centric direction. In addition to continuing to loosen up the muscles that'll help you get optimal rotation at the spine and hips, performing the movement in golf posture will prep your lower back for your upcoming eighteen holes.

How to do it   Assume golf posture while holding a club parallel to the ground at midthigh level. Your hands should be slightly wider than shoulders' width apart. See Picture 112.

Maintaining proper spine angle, twist to the right, keeping your arms straight. Turn your hips, pivot on the ball of your left foot, and imagine yourself staying in-plane while rotating. At the deepest point of the rotation, you want to be able to look straight down and see your left shoulder directly below your chin. See Picture 113.

Return to the address position, pause for a beat, then twist your upper body to the left. Again, maintain a proper spine angle, and to maximize rotation, pivot your right foot and go up on the ball of the foot. See Picture 114.

Do ten twists in each direction.

IV—CHEST, SHOULDER, AND TRICEPS STRETCH

115

A huge chunk of this program was spent opening up the chest and shoulders and getting your shoulders to rotate more. This stretch will wake up all the necessary body parts and let you take advantage of all the hard work you put in while you were fixing your body.

How to do it   Hold a golf club vertically behind your back. Your right hand should be at the top of the club with your right arm bent slightly. Your left hand should be near the clubhead at belt level. See Pictures 115 and 116.

116

Keeping the club vertical, perpendicular to the ground, and right along your spine, pull down gently with your left hand. This will cause your right arm to bend at the elbow. You should feel a nice stretch in your triceps in the back part of your right arm. See Pictures 117 and 118.

Return to the starting position to complete the rep. Do ten up-and-downs with your right hand on top, and then ten up-and-downs with your left hand on top.

117

118

V—OVERHEAD EXTENSION WITH CLUB

This stretch is another super way to open up the chest and loosen the shoulders. Start slowly with this one, but look to hit your maximum range of motion by the last few reps.

How to do it   Assume golf posture while holding a club parallel to the ground at midthigh level. Your arms should be extended in front of you with hands slightly wider than shoulders' width apart. See Picture 119.

Without losing your spine angle or the extension in your arms, raise the club over your head. See Picture 120. Hold for a beat, then return to the starting position with good golf posture to complete the rep.

Again, you're here to warm up, so take it slowly. Eventually shoot for getting your biceps up to your ears, but if your body doesn't feel ready for that on your first few reps, don't push it. It'll come.

119   **120**

VI—KNEELING HIP FLEXOR STRETCH

If you've got an early tee time and you've been sleeping, or if you've got an afternoon tee time and you've been sitting at your desk (or sleeping), then your hip flexors are probably going to be tight. Tight hip flexors will affect your posture and your ability to get your hips involved properly during your swing. We want to make sure that they're not tight.

How to do it   Kneel on the ground with your right knee and have your left leg in front of you with your left foot flat on the ground. Your posture should be good; your hips should be aligned directly over your right knee, and your shoulders should be aligned directly over your hips. Your left knee should be directly over your left heel. Hold a golf club off to your right side for support. See Picture 121.

Carefully step out about six inches with your left foot and push your hips forward. Your shoulders should still be aligned directly over your hips, but now if you drew a line straight down from your hips it would end up about six inches in front of your right knee. See Picture 122. You should feel this in the front of your right hip, at the top of your right leg. Return to the starting position to complete the rep.

Do ten reps with your left leg in the front, then ten with your right leg in the front.

FOOD FOR THOUGHT

In addition to making sure that your body is prepped for the movements it has to do, you must make it ready to do those movements consistently over eighteen holes. That's where proper fueling comes in. You have to feed your body correctly before and during a round to make sure it performs at its peak.

You have it easier than the pros when it comes to nutrition. You may play a round a week—maybe more, maybe less, depending on how lucky you are. Your livelihood doesn't depend on your playing your absolute best in four rounds on four consecutive days. My guess is that on those rare occasions when you have played four rounds over four days, it was on a long weekend with your buddies—a weekend that involved more than a few libations and some time in a "gentleman's club" or two. My God! Can you imagine if your income was tied into how well you played the back nine of your last round?

I am constantly on my guys about making sure they eat correctly before, during, and after they play when they're at a tournament. No matter how well they prepared themselves for Thursday's round, if they're out of gas by Sunday, they're going to plummet down the money list.

Fortunately, prepping for a single round is a lot easier and takes less time than prepping your nutrition for an entire tournament. This isn't a diet book. I'm not going to tell you how to lose thirty pounds or develop six-pack abs. I am going to tell what you should be putting in your body—and what you should avoid putting in your body—if you want to make the most of your time on the course. What you eat before you play will determine how much energy and focus you have when you start your round, and what you eat while playing will determine how sharp your game is when the match is on the line.

Just as you want your round of golf to start off strong, you want your day to start off strong. A lot of people sabotage themselves from the get-go by eating a less than optimal breakfast. If you grab a doughnut (or two), or one of those giant muffins that's the size of a chimp's head, then think that you've fueled yourself correctly because your stomach is temporarily full, it may be time to fix your diet so you can fix your swing. Starting your day with a lot of empty calories from white-flour- and white-sugar-based food is the equivalent of start-

> You spend seven straight weeks on the road, and if you're not doing the proper things to take care of your body, after about that fourth, fifth, or sixth week, not only are you sore, it's a struggle just to wake up. And when that happens, you're in a bad mood already. Your day's just not starting out good.
>
> —Travis Perkins, touring professional

ing your round with a drive into the woods and following it up with back-to-back shots into the water hazard.

I recommend getting the day off to a good start with a bowl of oatmeal. You can throw some nuts or raisins in and maybe add some low-fat or nonfat milk. You could also have some low-fat or nonfat cottage cheese. You want to give yourself some lean protein (from the cottage cheese), some quality, slow-burning carbohydrates (from the oatmeal), some faster-burning carbs (from the raisins), and a small amount of fat (from the nuts). Don't worry if that doesn't seem like a big breakfast. The key to maintaining energy, strength, and concentration is to fuel your body every two to three hours. You never find yourself overly hungry, and you never find yourself overly full. You're always good to go.

Once you're on the course, think of the food that you bring with you as the fifteenth club in your bag. You've probably done plenty of homework to make sure the first fourteen clubs in your bag are the best you can have. It should be no different with this fifteenth club.

Again, you're going to be eating small meals every couple of hours. Bring a turkey sandwich on multigrain bread with some mustard, a couple of pieces of fruit, and maybe a low-fat, low-sugar protein bar or two. Have a bar before you play, have half your sandwich and a piece of fruit somewhere in the front nine, have the rest of your sandwich during the back nine, and have another piece of fruit for energy for the last couple of holes. Both your energy and your focus will be strong and consistent throughout your entire game, and you'll be getting the most out of the body that you've worked so hard to get golf-ready. Who knows? Maybe when your buddies see you eating so well and playing so well, they'll do the math and realize that hot dogs and beer don't make for the best golf fuel.

That brings us to the next tip. You want to stay hydrated, but that doesn't mean you want to make repeated trips to the beer cart. The Joey D. Dozen does not refer to the number of beers you drink over eighteen holes. Try to avoid alcohol while you play. If you're going to drink, wait until you're done playing. First, alcohol is going to mess with your judgment and coordination, your ability to figure out distances, and your ability to read the greens. You'll end up trying to pull off shots that may work in video games, but don't usually work in the real world. Worse, you'll even start putting money on those asinine shots. And even though it's a liquid and can seem refreshing, alcohol will actually dehydrate you. It's also going to overload your system with a lot of calories that don't deliver much bang for the buck. Remember, quality calories over the course of your round are the key to consistent energy and focus. Empty calories, whether they come from hot dogs, candy bars, or beer, are big steps in the wrong direction.

Empty calories can also come from surprising sources. In addition to alcohol, you also should stay away from "sports drinks." These are basically just sugar water. A single bottle has around 150 calories—all coming from simple sugars. Drink three or four of those during your round and you're adding a whole lot of extra calories to your diet and seriously messing with your blood-sugar levels, which will affect your energy level. If you were running a sprint triathlon, where you were rapidly burning through your body's calorie stores, I might recommend a sports drink, but on the golf course your best bet is water. Drink more water than you think you need. If you're playing eighteen holes on a sunny afternoon, your body will need hydration before your brain tells you that you're thirsty.

You've worked hard off the course to get your body in the shape it needs to be in. On the course, the stretching you do to prepare your new golf body to play and the fuel you put into your new golf body will let you make the most of all of your hard work.

THE LAST WORD

Congratulations for taking the initiative to change your body. Most people aren't so forward-thinking. Most people are afraid to rip away the layers and get to the root of their problems. You boldly took a cold, hard look at your body—a body that you'd probably grown comfortable with—and decided that if you wanted to improve as a golfer, you were going to have to make some changes.

Change isn't easy. I bet you were at times frustrated by this program—you were doing things (or trying to do things) that your body either couldn't do or that it didn't want to do. You stuck with it, though, and I'm confident that you're now seeing the payoff from all of that work.

My guess is that you have golfing buddies who still think that the solution to their slices, hooks, and flimsy hundred-yard drives is a new driver or a new stance. Hopefully, your example will show them that you sometimes have to dig a little bit deeper to fix what's wrong. Only when you discover the real root of the problem can you ever hope to truly solve the problem. The amazing part is that this doesn't just apply to your golf swing. If you were able to cure a decades-old slice, imagine what else you can fix when you're not afraid to discover the real root of the problem. But I don't mean to get all philosophical on you—I'm just a biomechanics coach.

Appendix

If you're looking for more information about Joey Diovisalvi, or to order any of the equipment you may need, go to www.golfgym.com.

If you're looking for more information about Steve Steinberg and his studio, go to www.blackbeltfitness.com.